GUITARS, BARS, AND MOTOWN SUPERSTARS

GUITARS, BARS, AND MOTOWN SUPERSTARS

DENNIS COFFEY

University of Michigan Press

Ann Arbor

Dedicated to my children

Jordan, Denise, Dennis, James, and Andrew

First paperback edition 2009
Copyright © by Dennis Coffey 2004
All rights reserved
Published in the United States of America by
The University of Michigan Press
Manufactured in the United States of America
⊚ Printed on acid-free paper

2012   2011   2010   2009   5   4   3   2

A CIP catalog record for this book is available from the British Library.

Library of Congress Cataloging-in-Publication Data
Coffey, Dennis.
    Guitars, bars, and Motown superstars / Dennis Coffey.
        p.   cm.
      ISBN 0-472-11399-2 (cloth : alk. paper)
        1. Coffey, Dennis.   2. Guitarists—United States—Biography.   3.
    Rock musicians—United States—Biography.   I. Title.
    ML419.C62A3   2004
    787.87'166'092—dc22   2003026182

ISBN-13: 978-0-472-03410-9 (pbk. : alk. paper)
ISBN-10: 0-472-03410-3 (pbk. : alk. paper)

Acknowledgments

The idea of writing a book has always fascinated me. As a child, I read every book I could get my hands on, riding my bicycle to the public library in Detroit to take home three or four at a time. When I was young, I never dreamed of writing a book, but as I got older I knew I would.

I would like to thank my mom, Gertrude Schultz, for raising my sister Pat and me, even though she had the dreams and talent to be a writer and singer.

The second person to thank is my good friend of over twenty years, Charles Kipps. Charles was a songwriter and record producer and is now a successful writer and TV producer. He was my mentor and patiently answered all of my questions and gave me valuable advice. It was very difficult to write my first book, but Charles kept my spirits up and encouraged me to stay with it.

Next I would like to thank Ted Brichze. Ted was a food and beverage manager at a large hotel in the Metro Detroit area. He listened to my endless stories about the music business and kept saying, "You should write a book."

"If I do," I always said, "I'll give you credit in the front pages."

I would also like to thank David Flynn for the support he has given me in getting my book published. A special thanks to Stuart Russell and Mike Ritson of BeeCool Publishing in London and Chris Hebert of the University of Michigan Press. Also a special thanks to Susan Whitall and Millie Felch for believing in my book.

Finally, I would like to dedicate this book to the studio musicians everywhere who work tirelessly in the background to create the music that lifts the spirit and touches the soul.

Contents

Music is the sound track of your life.
DICK CLARK

Early Years

DETROIT, MICHIGAN, 1940S

I was raised in a single-parent family in Detroit, a city famous for two things—automobiles and great music. We lived in a middle-class neighborhood on a street lined with tall, shady elm and oak trees. Our house was a white wooden bungalow with asbestos siding and no basement. Under the house was a crawl space where my mom used to wash clothes. It was surrounded by dirt walls and had plenty of creepy crawlies coming out of the ground. When I was young, I was afraid to go down there because it was so damp and scary. Our house also had an unfinished attic. I sometimes played up there, but the attic was just a wooden floor with no paneling.

My mom, Gertrude Schultz, was very attractive, with brown hair and blue eyes. She combed her hair in the style of the forties, with curls in the front and back and a pageboy cut around the sides. Mom had the soul of a big band singer. I remember her playing the piano like mad and singing the big band songs of the era on weekends—"Slow Boat To China" and "Am I Blue"—while she did her housework. Mom had an excellent voice and should have been a professional singer.

My mom was born in Copper City, a small town of three hundred souls on the Keweenaw Peninsula at the northern tip of Upper

Michigan—the heart of the "Copper Country." Copper City was a real rough and tumble mining community in the late 1800s and early 1900s, before most of the copper ore ran out.

Mom came down to Detroit from Copper City at the age of eighteen. She worked as a domestic so that she wouldn't be a financial drain on her father up north, even though my grandfather was a successful businessman at the time. Mom learned to be frugal in those early years and still is to this day. That's how we survived. Her motto was always "waste not, want not," and she practiced what she preached. It was very difficult for me to understand why my mother left the spacious and beautiful Copper Country to live in Detroit, but she was very independent and there were simply no jobs for a young girl of eighteen in the man's world of logging and mining up north.

My mom raised me and my sister Pat alone, and to this day I still don't know how she managed it. Years later my sister Pat would do the same, raising two kids as a single parent. In those days, our family ate a lot of leftovers, but we always had good solid food on the table. We owned our own home, and both the house and our clothes were always clean. Even though money was tight, we still had treats like potato chips and soda pop as we watched television on Saturday nights.

Although we got a TV set soon after they were available, I remember that our neighbors down the street had the first television on the block. All of the kids in the neighborhood used to go down to their house once a week to watch the puppet show *Kukla, Fran, and Ollie*.

I used to watch television on Saturday nights with my mom and Pat. We liked *Our Show of Shows* with Sid Caesar, *The Jackie Gleason Show*, *The Ted Mack Original Amateur Hour*, *The Hit Parade*, and *Lawrence Welk*. Even back then I envied the musicians on those shows. I listened to their music and watched their every move. We would sit in front of the television, eat our potato chips, drink pop, and laugh hysterically most of the night. I didn't feel any different from anyone else my age living on our street. We were a close-knit family and pretty much had what everyone else did in our blue-collar neighborhood.

Because my parents got divorced when my dad came home from

World War II, we never had a father on a regular basis. Life on the weekends was pretty boring. I used to ride my bike to local parks and movie matinees with friends, so I learned to be pretty self-reliant in those days. We didn't own a car until I was twelve.

My father, James Coffey, along with his nine brothers and sisters, was raised in a small farmhouse in the hills of Kentucky. I imagine his childhood being like a scene from the movie *Tobacco Road*, with my grandfather eking out a living as a coal miner and owing his soul to the company store.

"He never received a check from working in the mine that I know of," my dad told me once, sadly shaking his head. "And if any coal miner paid off the company store and asked for a paycheck from the owners of the mine, they were immediately fired."

When the mine ran out of coal, my grandfather eventually hitched a train ride up to Detroit to find work. When he had saved enough money for train fare, he brought my dad and the rest of the family up north. That's how the Coffey family was relocated.

I came from a musical family on my mother's side. My mother and my aunts played the piano and sang. At the age of thirteen, I went on a trip to visit my grandmother and the rest of my relatives in Copper City in northern Michigan. It was on that trip that I first became enchanted with the guitar. Jim and Marilyn Thompson, my cousins, were playing guitar and singing country music, and as I watched them I became totally fascinated. They were willing to show me how to play and got me started. Now I finally had a use for the old guitar that had been sitting in the closet at home, gathering dust, since my mother's boyfriend Harold gave it to me.

Growing up in Detroit, I had a lot of time to practice guitar. My mom worked all day, and I saw my dad only about three times a year: Easter, Christmas, and my birthday. In those days, I usually had to entertain myself, especially on weekends and in the summer when there was no school.

I began by learning to strum chords while singing country songs. My favorite artist at the time was Hank Williams. After my cousins, my teachers were anyone who knew more about playing guitar than I did. With both passion and intensity, I focused on one thing—learning everything I possibly could.

As a teenager, I studied country, rockabilly, rock & roll, rhythm & blues, blues, and jazz. My major influences were guitarists Scotty Moore (with Elvis), James Burton (with Ricky Nelson), B. B. King, Chuck Berry, and Wes Montgomery. Chuck was playing some guitar licks so innovative that I couldn't even imagine what the hell he was doing. But after a while I finally got good enough to imitate some of his guitar parts by listening to his records and playing along. Chuck Berry, almost singlehandedly, started a rock & roll guitar army across the country. I was practicing relentlessly. I didn't care if it took me a whole week to learn one song or one riff, I persisted until I got better and better.

As a teenager, I attended Mackenzie High in Detroit. One day when I was in the tenth grade I decided to play guitar and sing in the school auditorium at a student assembly. On the day of the assembly, I came to school with my little amplifier and my new electric guitar ready to kick ass. Actually, I was as nervous as hell. I was wearing my infamous George Raft-style white flannel suit with a black shirt and my thin yellow knit tie and blue suede shoes.

The assembly began, and the teachers made their announcements to a sedate student body. When they were through with the introductions, they introduced me—"The Rock & Roll Kid"! After the introduction, I walked out on the stage, plugged my guitar into my amplifier, and looked out into the audience. It suddenly hit me like a ton of bricks: I was up here in front of all these people by myself—under the spotlight. The only sound I heard was the pounding of my heart and my rapid breathing. Well, rock & roll was never for the fainthearted, so I just cranked up the volume of my amplifier and let 'er rip.

"Well, it's one for the money, two for the show," I sang, from a song written by Carl Perkins. "Three to get ready, now go Kat go. But don't you . . . step on my blue suede shoes. You can do anything, but honey lay off of them shoes!"

My eyes were closed and I was really jamming. I put my heart and soul into the music, and I could feel the kids going berserk just like they did in those early Alan Freed rock & roll movies. Suddenly my performance came to a screeching halt, followed by a deadly silence. I looked around and couldn't figure out what the hell had happened. I had been performing to a packed house, having the time of my life, and now there was nothing! I looked offstage, and the picture became very clear. I saw a teacher standing in the wings, holding my amplifier plug in her hand and beckoning me to leave the stage. The kids were clapping wildly for more, but when they saw the teacher with the amplifier plug in her hand they figured out what had happened. They began to hiss and boo. I felt like a fool just standing there, so I shook my head, turned around, and walked off the stage.

Once I reached the floor, I was confronted by the teacher, an older woman peering at me through Coke-bottle glasses. She was a large woman with a robust physique and a bad attitude.

"Young man," she hissed in a cold fury, her jaws tighter than a Spanish woodpecker's lips, "what was the meaning of that obscene demonstration?"

"What are you talking about?" I said, looking her right in the eye.

"You were up there on that stage waving that guitar around like a phallic symbol in front of all these kids, and I won't tolerate it," she said angrily. "You'll never, ever be allowed to perform at a school assembly again, you nasty boy!"

I was in a state of shock and disbelief. I thought I'd done a good job up there. After all, the kids had loved it. I just stood there, holding my guitar in my hand with my head down.

A shrivelled old spinster who was probably still a virgin had shut down "The Rock & Roll Kid" in his major debut. The teacher was still standing there yelling at me, using terms I didn't understand. I didn't even know the meaning of the word *phallic* until I looked it up in the school dictionary. At the time, I was only fourteen, not exactly Mr. Sexual Sophistication.

After the incident at the assembly, I kept a low profile at school events for a while, but you can't keep a good man—or "The Rock & Roll Kid"—down for long. Eventually, I started a rock & roll band, and we appeared at basketball games, which were not routinely attended by frustrated, narrow-minded, old maids. The kids at the games always clapped and went nuts when we performed because there weren't many bands around at that time that could play rock & roll. We were good even without all the special guitar effects you hear today, like distortion devices and digital echo. In fact, no one in Detroit even had an electric bass. They were all still using upright basses.

One day after school I received a telephone call from a singer by the name of Vic Gallon. He asked me to put together a band to accompany him on two songs he was recording. I quickly agreed, and hired two other musicians, Larry Blockno to play drums and Lee Stage to play bass guitar. Vic promised us fifteen dollars per song and said it would take about two hours of our time in the studio.

Lee Stage was twenty-three. I first met him when he answered an ad I placed in the newspaper for a bass player. Lee worked at a tough hillbilly bar on Woodward in Downtown Detroit. He was always accompanied by a nice-looking girlfriend who kept a nickel-plated .25 caliber automatic in her purse. Larry Blockno was a muscular, blond, blue-eyed kid of Polish descent who played the drums in my rock & roll band at school.

On the day of the session, we met Vic at a small basement studio on the northwest side of Detroit. He greeted us warmly and played his songs on a guitar while he sang. We had never heard the songs until that day. There was no music, so we began to create the parts we would play on the record.

Vic was a short, chubby guy in dark blue work pants and matching T-shirt. He had a blue-collar day job, a good rockabilly voice, and the desire to record and release his own record. I was excited because it was the first time I had ever been in a real recording studio. As an extra incentive, I was going to get paid as well. Vic never mentioned how he got my phone number, but I was determined to do the best job that I possibly could.

Vic counted off the first song, an upbeat rockabilly tune named "I'm Gone," and began singing and strumming rhythm guitar. I played rockabilly finger style in the verses, while Larry added a strong drumbeat and Lee followed along with a solid bass line. In the middle of the song, I kicked out a super raunchy guitar solo, which sounded like a cross between early Roy Orbison and Elvis era Scotty Moore. I still listen to that solo once in a while. It sounded authentic in the style of the fifties, and considering I was only fifteen at the time it was damned impressive!

We kept recording the first song until Vic listened to the playback one last time and agreed it was a final take.

"Great guys, that's a take!" he said, grinning from ear to ear, excited to have heard his song on tape. "Now, let's go on to the next song. It's a country ballad called "I'll Keep Lovin' You."

Vic counted off the song and played his guitar. I created a riff in the introduction that Vic thought was fantastic; he used it again in the middle of the song. After a few takes, we finally got the one he was looking for.

"Man that sounds sweet," Vic said. "This is gonna be a number one record! You guys can pack up your stuff. We're all done. Dennis, come on in the control room and listen to the playback."

The recording studio itself was in the basement. There were soundproof materials on the walls to keep the traffic noise out and sound baffles to separate the sounds between the different instruments. The control room was in a booth in one corner of the basement. I went inside and was amazed by all the buttons and audio equipment, especially the large tape recorder attached to the wall. It was quite a contrast to the little tinny-sounding tape recorder I had at home. The recording engineer played the tape, and I listened to the music. I was really impressed at how good it sounded and noticed that the engineer had added heavy tape delay echo as well.

"Hey man, that's a great sound. I can hear it on the radio already," I said with genuine enthusiasm.

"Thanks man. You guys all did a fantastic job," Vic answered. "Here's what I owe you."

Vic gave me the money for the session. I kept my share and paid Larry and Lee.

"You guys sounded great," I added. "I hope we can do this again."

Vic promised to give me a copy of the record when it came out.

What a great way to make money, I said to myself. You jam your ass off playing guitar with other musicians and have a great time in the process. And when it's over you get thirty dollars for two hours' work. What a hell of a deal!

Later Vic sent me a disc jockey copy of the record on his label, Gondola. I played it on my hi fidelity record player at home and I was in musical heaven! It was the first time I'd ever heard myself play guitar on a record.

A few days later Vic called me up again.

"Hey, Dennis," he said excitedly. "Listen to country radio station WEXL tomorrow at four in the afternoon. I'm going to be interviewed and get the record played."

I told him I wouldn't miss it for anything.

I was so excited that I could hardly sleep that night. I was actually going to hear myself play guitar on the radio.

The next day I turned on the station with the volume up full blast. Sure enough, Vic came on the air and introduced us as the backup musicians. Then the DJ played both songs. Man, when I heard myself playing, I felt great. What a rush! I was addicted.

Unfortunately, the record we'd made wasn't properly promoted so it never sold a lot of copies. "I'm Gone" wasn't picked up by a major label either, which was too bad, because it could have really done something. Vic and the rest of us thought it had a chance to make it big.

I still have that record. In fact, in 1991, a record collector drove all the way up to Detroit from Columbus, Ohio, and offered to buy it from me, but I wouldn't sell.

"How in the hell did you find out about a record on a hometown label that only released one record and only pressed about four hundred copies in Ohio?" I asked the collector.

He explained that someone he knew worked at a record-pressing plant in Indianapolis. They'd found a copy and thought it was an excellent example of the rockabilly of that period.

Back in 1955 I couldn't have imagined that more than thirty years later people would still remember the record. I also had no way of knowing, as I basked in the glow of my newfound musical success, that in a small studio hidden in the shadows of Wayne State University in midtown Detroit I would soon meet a visionary who would make such an impact on the music scene that the music world would never be the same.

Makin' Records

The first time I met Berry Gordy, I was sixteen and Berry was the arranger and producer on a recording session. The artists were me and a rockabilly singer named Durwood Hutto. Durwood was an Elvis look-alike who performed with a powerful, electrifying voice, wild gyrating hip movements, slicked-down, coal-black hair, and long sideburns. The girls went wild over him whenever we performed.

Durwood and I appeared many times as a duo playing the USO club in Downtown Detroit, at private parties, and in halls. Our audiences always rewarded us with plenty of applause. When you're sixteen and just starting out, that kind of response in itself can be pretty exciting. I played lead electric guitar and sang harmony while Durwood strummed away like crazy on a big, blond acoustic Gibson guitar and belted out the lead vocals. We definitely got it on with our music and had a hell of a good time doing it. We also met lots of chicks, which gave us even more incentive to play.

Durwood lived in a big, ten-story brownstone building on LaSalle Street, close to Grand Boulevard in the Motor City. We used to get together at his apartment and write songs when we weren't out performing. One of the songs we wrote together was called "Crazy Little Satellite," about the Russians sending the first satellite, Sputnik, into orbit.

One day we decided to make a demo of our song and try to get a record deal. After all, we reasoned, Paul Anka was only fifteen when he made it big. We asked around to see if anyone knew of a cheap recording studio. We didn't have much money at the time. Someone suggested Fortune Recording Studios, which was also the home of Fortune Records.

Fortune Studios was a dinky, rundown recording studio in an old brown building on Third Avenue in the Cass Corridor in Detroit. We drove up to the studio, parked my mom's red Ford sedan on the street, and went inside. We paid the fee and recorded our song that day. When we were done, a woman named Devora Brown, who was one of the owners, asked to hear the tape. To our surprise, she offered us a record contract with her and Nat Tarnapol, Jackie Wilson's manager and producer at the time. Although the events leading up to the recording contract are a little vague after all these years, some things still remain perfectly clear.

We were introduced to Nat and given a contract to sign. We were both so young that our parents had to cosign with us. Given our lack of experience, we didn't even consider having a lawyer look at it. After we signed, Nat started the wheels in motion to cut a record on us and lease it to a major record label.

First Nat sent us to rehearse at a house on Brush Street in Downtown Detroit. He told us when we got there to ask for Berry Gordy or Billy Davis. They would provide the musicians to rehearse the songs. By that time, we had written two. These musicians would also play on the recording session.

I remember putting my black, electric, solid-body Premier guitar and a small amplifier in the trunk of my mom's red '52 Ford, and we headed downtown. In those days we were young, full of teenage enthusiasm, and thought nothing of driving all over Detroit or the suburbs to play our music. We were both totally fascinated by the new combination of hillbilly and rock & roll known as rockabilly. We loved everything that came out of Sun Records in Memphis, and we played every song Elvis ever made. I would drive anywhere to hear a new guitar player. I also practiced night and day and learned all of the guitar licks and solos that were being played on the radio.

The first time I met Berry Gordy was at the rehearsal house. It was a beautiful two-story brick house off of Brush Street. A guitar player, drummer, and piano player were sitting in the living room ready to practice with us before the session. The musicians were already in tune, so we tuned up our guitars with the piano and waited for Berry.

A few minutes later, Berry came downstairs, smiled, and introduced himself. He was wearing dark brown slacks and a white polo shirt. Berry was very friendly and treated us real nice. Being two teenagers who had just signed our first recording contract, we didn't quite know what to expect.

At that time, I had no way of knowing that Berry would later start his own record company and that I would be one of his studio musicians. I wonder if when I worked for him later he even remembered the two young white boys who had wanted to become recording stars and rehearsed in the living room of his house. He probably never knew that the guitarist Motown used on so many hit records was the same person. I never mentioned it to anyone the entire time I worked at Motown.

We rehearsed our two songs with the band, and, although I was still a little nervous, I was impressed with the knowledge and talent of both Berry Gordy and the musicians. They really seemed to know their stuff. We practiced our songs over and over until we got them down real smooth. Then Berry ended the rehearsal and told us to be ready to record the songs tomorrow night at United Sound Studios on Second Avenue across from Wayne State University.

The next night, I borrowed my mother's car again, picked up Durwood at his apartment, and headed over to the recording studio. I parked the car on a side street and went in the front door. United Sound Studios was located in a large two-story brick house, which also had sound- and film-editing rooms on the second floor. There was also a small recording studio in the front of the building and a large soundstage for filming in the back, which had been converted into a recording studio. When we entered the studio, Berry Gordy and the musicians were already there, so we set up our equipment and placed the lyrics on a music stand in front of us. We didn't want to forget the words.

Berry counted off the tempo to the first song, and we belted out the main hook in two-part harmony: "Crazy little satellite running wild, Crazy little satellite running wild . . ." Durwood and I banged away at our guitars and sang in harmony like the Everly Brothers.

We sang our songs over and over until we were almost tired of them. I say "almost" because in truth we were so excited that the studio probably could have blown up and melted before we'd got tired of recording our own music. We kept singing until we finally got a performance that was acceptable to Berry. Our song "Crazy Little Satellite" sounded stupid, but it was written when songs titled "Purple People Eater" and "Ooo Mow Mow" were big hits.

That was my first recording session as an artist and my second time in the studio. Until then I'd been recording music at home on a tape recorder. We were young, inexperienced, and nervous in the studio, but we made up for it with enthusiasm and by playing our hearts out. We had stars in our eyes and were determined to make it big.

After our session was over, the recording engineer made an acetate upstairs on a cutting lathe. We left the studio feeling euphoric—we were on our way to stardom! We laughed and joked and told each other we would be on *American Bandstand* in about three months. We were ready.

At about eleven o'clock, Durwood and I walked out of the studio and headed for my mother's car. The street was dark and deserted, but in those days it wasn't as dangerous as it is now. I had my car keys in my hand, and Durwood was carrying the dub of our new record. I walked up to my car and placed the key in the lock, but I couldn't seem to get it to go in. I was still trying to make the key fit when I heard the sound of running feet behind me. I turned around just in time to see this big maniac charging down on me. Bam! He hit me with a vicious karate chop right where my shoulder met my neck, and I dropped to the ground like a sack of dead meat. Then the crazy bastard jumped on me and dragged me up by my shirt.

"Did you think you could get away with stealing my car?!" He was screaming in my face. Veins were popping out on his forehead.

"What the hell are you talking about?" I yelled back. "Here, look, I have the keys in my hand. This is my car!"

By then I was in shock, but I still managed to look past him up the street. That was when I saw my car sitting two parking spaces down. My car matched his exactly. It was the same model and the same color.

"Hey," I yelled. "Hold on! My car is behind you on the street. Can you see it? It looks just like yours. It was an honest mistake."

Just as the maniac was getting ready to make jelly out of my face, he saw what had happened. He let go and stopped punching me.

"Hell, I'm sorry kid," he said. "I thought you were trying to steal my car. I just got back from the Korean War. I was in the Marines, and I guess I'm still a little edgy. I'm attending night school here at Wayne State, trying to get a degree."

He turned and climbed into his car and drove away.

I wasn't sorry to see him go. I've never seen a guy move so fast and inflict so much damage so quickly. I figured that's probably how he survived the Korean War. Badly shaken but unbowed, Durwood and I headed home from our first record date, none the worse for the wear and tear.

Six months went by.

We kept asking when our record was going to be released, but all we seemed to be getting from the producers was the runaround. Each time I called they couldn't come up with a release date. Finally, we got discouraged and decided to ask for our record contract back. When I called and asked for our contract I was told that Nat Tarnapol had it and that we would need to see him about it.

Durwood and I decided to pay Nat a visit at his upstairs office on Woodward Avenue, off Alexandrine in Detroit. I drove Downtown, parked my mom's car on Woodward, and we walked up to the office building. We went upstairs and entered Nat's office. It looked sleazy and messy, like the office of some TV private eye. It gave me the creeps.

Nat was sitting at the desk in his office when we walked in and sat down.

"Hi Nat," I said. "We were told there still isn't a release date for our record and we don't believe it's ever coming out. We want our contract back."

Nat looked up at us in surprise and then seemed to give our request some thought. "No! I'm sorry," he said, "a contract's a contract whether the record is released or not. I'm sure it will come out in due time."

Durwood, a pretty big country boy, stood up kind of red-faced and hot under the collar. He stared down at Nat for a brief minutes before an evil look came over his face.

"Nat, we understand just fine," he said gravely, "so I guess I'll jus' have to whup your ass!"

Durwood lunged for Nat and just missed as Nat reached for the telephone to call the police. Quick as a cat, Durwood reached across the desk and pulled the telephone cord out of the wall. Suddenly Nat had a change of heart.

"OK, OK, you boys calm down," he said nervously. "You can have your contract back!"

Nat shoved his hand into his desk drawer and pulled out a packet of paper.

"If you guys are going to get nuts about it, here's your damn contract," he muttered as he reached across the desk and handed it to me.

"Thanks," we said, as we turned and walked out of his office.

As we drove away, Durwood turned to me, smiled with a glint in his eye, and muttered, "Did you see that son of a bitch come up with our contract when I pulled the phone out of the wall? If he hadn't of, I would've punched his lights out. That's how we handle his kind down home."

About six months later I got a telephone call from Billy Davis, Berry's partner.

"Me and Berry are starting our own record company, and we want to know if you and Durwood would be interested in recording for us."

By now, we had both had enough of the record business, so I wasn't about to jump back into it.

"Thanks, but no thanks," I said. "I think I've had about enough of the record business for the time being."

I think that day must have been the beginning of Motown Records.

After I got over that experience, I answered an ad in the paper for a lead guitarist for a weekend band. I was sixteen and continued to use my mom's maroon Ford to go to auditions. The following Saturday I went to try out for the job in Garden City.

The name of the band was the Rhythm Kings, which was later changed to the Pyramids. The leader of the band was Val Gursky, who sang and played accordion and electric piano. His brother Bob played drums. We jammed on a few songs, and they hired me on the spot. The band played weddings on Saturday nights and teen clubs on Friday nights.

There was a circuit of teen clubs in the area, and about twenty teenage bands worked steadily, gaining valuable experience for future careers in music. A lot of musicians, including me, would later work full time when the bars finally changed over from the music of the forties to rock & roll. Of course, that was after we turned twenty-one.

On my new job with the Rhythm Kings, I was paid fifteen dollars each night for a grand total of thirty dollars per week. Prior to this I'd had to work all week after school as a cashier in a supermarket for just fifteen dollars a week, so I considered this job a real opportunity. Plus I was excited to get paid to do something I loved as much as music. I probably would have done it for nothing!

But all good things must come to an end. Once I graduated from high school, I had to look for a full-time job. Playing on the weekends with a kiddy band just didn't work for an eighteen year old. At the time, only two clubs were booking rock & roll bands as entertainment, Rose's Bar on Vernor in Southwest Detroit, and the Pullman Lounge in Dearborn. But you had to be able to prove you were twenty-one to work at either place.

I looked in the newspaper for jobs and applied at a few factories, but there were no jobs for an eighteen-year-old guitar player with no other skills. In 1959, there were still plenty of grown men with experience, and they took all unskilled jobs that were out there. Having nothing else to do, I took my dad's place for two weeks at the Sealtest Ice Cream plant in Detroit while he went on vacation. But after he came back I was out of work again.

In those days, with the draft in effect, I knew I would have to serve sooner or later. Since I wasn't doing much of anything anyway, I decided to get it over with. At one of the weddings I played, I'd met a guy who had been in the paratroopers. He'd told me what badasses they were. I thought, what the hell, if I was going to join the Army I might as well volunteer for the airborne and make the fifty-five dollars a month extra in jump pay.

My dad had other ideas. He'd been in the Navy during World War II, and even though he'd lost a lung when a German U-boat torpedoed his ship he still wanted me to go into the Navy.

"In the Navy," he said, "you always had three warm meals a day and a place to sleep." Maybe so, but I knew if I joined the Marines, Navy, or Air Force, I'd have to enlist for three years. But if I volunteered for the draft I'd be out in two. I opted for the Army.

My dad took me down to the Army Recruiting Office. They tried their damnedest to get me to sign up for three years, but I wasn't buying it.

"Even if you volunteered for the draft right now," the recruiter said, "we probably couldn't take you for months. But if you enlisted for three years, we could take you immediately."

"That's OK," I said. "I'll take my chances with the draft."

Of course, they drafted me right away, and I was riding on a train to Fort Leonard Wood, Missouri, within two weeks. I was heading into the unknown and beginning a new adventure.

My new adventure was as a paratrooper in the 101st Airborne Division, where I tested my courage and learned a lot about myself. I had been in the Army just a couple of months when I began jump school. Six months after I graduated from jump school, I was in town playing guitar one night and almost missed a field maneuver the next morning. Having almost been court-martialed as a result, I decided that would be a good time to leave the 101st.

My final assignment led me to Columbia, South Carolina, where I had a chance to play guitar in the recording studio and the clubs when I wasn't playing army.

Sweet Southern Soul Music

COLUMBIA, SOUTH CAROLINA, 1961

After I left the 101st and took a leave back in Detroit, I spent the rest of my army career at Fort Jackson in Columbia, South Carolina. There, while playing guitar with a band at a bar called the Sputnik Club, off the highway on the outskirts of town, I met my first wife, Joyce. The Sputnik Club was a one-story cinder block building with bullet holes in the ceiling. The owner was Jim, a formidable, grizzled man in his forties who was as rough and tough looking as his club.

I'll never forget the Sputnik Club. In addition to being the place where I met Joyce, it was also the place where my music career was almost over before it began. It was the first—but not the last—time in my life that someone pointed a gun at me and actually threatened to shoot me.

I had just completed a set and was standing outside taking a smoke break when I looked over and saw this little shrimp of a guy hassling this huge character, who was doing his best to ignore him. Was this shrimp crazy, I wondered, or does he have some kind of inner need to get his ass kicked? I had the feeling that if the little guy didn't shut up, that need was going to be met real fast. Sure enough, the big guy finally lost his patience and knocked the shrimp out with one punch. He then turned around and walked back into the club without even working up a sweat. The little guy crumpled up like an old dishrag, fell facedown on the cement sidewalk, and lay there.

In the past, when I was hired out to play music, I had learned to mind my own business. You live a lot longer that way. I finished my cigarette and was about to walk back into the club when suddenly I heard a car pull up out of nowhere and screech to a stop. The door flew open and a wild-looking guy in a tan trench coat raced up to me and pointed a gigantic .22 caliber revolver right in my face.

"Did you beat up my buddy over there?" he yelled.

When someone points a real, loaded gun in your face, and if you have an ounce of brains, it scares the crap right out of you. Forget about the TV show hype where the local hero jumps the bad guy and takes his gun away even though the bad guy has the drop on him. That was the last thing on my mind. I stared with terror at the ominous opening in the barrel of the gun—no way! I just wanted to get the hell out of there with the same body parts—and in the same condition—as when I'd come outside.

"Hey man—I didn't touch him," I said as my heart was doing flip-flops.

"The guy that punched him out is a big guy wearing a white shirt. He just went back into the club. Trust me, I had nothing to do with it. In fact, I don't even know what they were fighting about."

The guy with the gun must have believed me because he turned around and charged into the club.

I waited outside for a while and heard a commotion coming from the front door of the club. I looked over and saw the same guy in the trench coat backing out of the door with his hand in his pocket. I could see the barrel of the gun sticking out of a ragged hole pointed directly at Jim, the owner, who was pushing him through the door with one hand.

"Get the hell out of my club, you bastard," Jim was threatening, "and if you shoot me with that gun in your pocket, I'll kill you!"

At that time, I realized why no one ever caused Jim much trouble in his club. After that, I decided to find a safer environment in which to play.

My new gig turned out to be the Noncommissioned Officer's

Service Club, where I was allowed to go after being promoted to corporal. I sat in at the service club and played guitar with a band one night. As a result, the band offered me a job playing and recording with them. The piano player, John McCullough, and his partner had just produced a national hit record, "Stay," by a local group called Maurice Williams & the Zodiacs.

I really hit it off with these guys and spent every free moment I had with them, either at the club or in the recording studio. I even signed a record contract with Col Pix Records and released a single with the band playing backup. Col Pix made me change my name to Clark Summit because they told me an artist with a weird name like Dennis Coffey could never be a star. They didn't know that's exactly what would happen in the future.

The record they released was a song I wrote called "Holding Hands." I had high hopes for the record, but it didn't sell. So, when I was finally discharged from the Army in July, Joyce and I went back to Detroit to seek my fortune in the music business.

DETROIT, AUGUST 1961

We arrived in Detroit in the middle of a hot, muggy summer. The nights were wet and sticky, the days were hot and blistering, and the sidewalks reflected intense heat in shimmering waves like a mirage in a desert movie. We decided to stay at my mom's house on Greenlawn in Detroit, across from the railroad tracks and down the street from the city incinerator, until we got settled in. I had a new wife to support and no job prospects, but I was damned glad to be a free man again and excited to be home in the Motor City—the city of cars and bars, where the fights were frequent and the city was poppin'. I had very little savings, so I went down to the Michigan Employment Security Commission (MESC) and applied for unemployment. The following day, I called my old music buddies to see what was going on and to try to find work.

As a result of my phone calls, I received a call from my friend Marcus Terry, who played drums at the Wayne Show Bar in Wayne, Michigan. Marcus, a tall, curly headed blond from the South, was an excellent drummer, and would later tour all over the world with guitarist and singer Jose Feliciano. Marcus told me they were looking for a guitar player to work with the band.

"Would you be interested in coming down and playing an audition?" he asked.

"No problem," I answered. "Hell, it seems I've been playing auditions all my life to get work. I'll be there."

The Wayne Show Bar was located in an old building on Michigan Avenue, close to the small downtown area. As you walked in the front door there was a row of seats surrounding the bar in front of a raised stage on the right and additional seats and booths on the left. The band played on the stage behind the bar and was highly visible from anywhere in the room. In the old days, the Wayne Show Bar featured various entertainers and popular show bands from the area.

On the day of the audition, Marcus introduced me to the rest of the guys in the band. They were there to rehearse some new songs. I noticed a few early drinkers in the audience. It was only eleven o'clock in the morning. I was still pretty pumped up from playing all those gigs in the army and had a new wife to support, so I really gave it my best shot. Marcus called me the following day and offered me the job, which I instantly accepted.

I'd been out of the army for only two weeks, and I already had my first full-time job offer as a musician. I'd get ninety dollars for playing six nights a week. At the time, most factory workers made about one hundred dollars per week, so I felt it was a great start. I was amazed that I would actually get paid to do what I loved to do the most—play guitar.

The bar scene in Metropolitan Detroit was really kicking ass in 1961. Rock & roll was still in its infancy and spreading to the bars like wildfire. Before the birth of rock & roll, most bars featured show tunes, standards of the forties, or country and western. I was lucky to be playing music at a time when the rules were being broken every day. Loud, rude-sounding music that was worshiped by the young and was taking over the country by storm.

In the early years, rock & roll was a combination of rhythm & blues, gospel, swing, and country, and people couldn't seem to get enough of it. I was first aware of the popularity of rock & roll when a trickle of young white kids began to visit two bars in different sections of town—Rose's Bar in Detroit and the Pullman Lounge in Dearborn. This trickle soon grew into a torrential flood, and because of it many of my musician friends from the teen clubs began to make a living playing rock & roll in bars all over the city.

The young players in Detroit used the bars as a rich, fertile environment in which to sharpen their musical chops. The bars were also a meeting place where young musicians could socialize and network. When I lived on Stoeple Avenue in Detroit in the sixties, soul diva Aretha Franklin was playing piano and singing at the Stadium Bar on Puritan Avenue. Later, in the nineties, I saw Bob Seger hanging out in a bar on Woodward in Royal Oak called The Jukebox. I'd also run into jazz guitarist Earl Klugh from time to time at Mr. B's in Troy.

For a few years I was content working in bar bands and playing in clubs around town, and then one day I got a call to audition for a gig with saxophone player George Katsakis and a group called the Royaltones. I got the job, and George and I have been good friends ever since.

The Royaltones had had a few national instrumental hit records in the late fifties, "Poor Boy" and "Flamingo Express." They'd appeared on *American Bandstand* with Dick Clark. At the time I began working with them, they were playing in a bar on Fort Street called the Scenic Inn.

After I had played with the band for a while, George and I began writing songs together, and he introduced me to record producers Harry Balk and Irving McConnick, who recorded hits on Little Willie John, Johnny and the Hurricanes, Don & Juan, the Volumes, and Del Shannon. Harry and Irving owned Embee Productions and Twirl and Impact Records. Harry was one of the first successful record producers I had ever met. He always smoked these huge cigars and spoke with a New York accent. In his later years, Harry worked for Motown.

One of the main songwriters for Harry and Irving at the time was Duke Browner. Duke wrote and produced songs for the Volumes and some of Harry Balk's other groups, while T.J. Fowler and Motown Funk Brother, piano player Joe Hunter wrote the musical arrangements. Duke wrote some good songs, but he had one major eccentricity: when he played his songs on the piano, he'd use only the black keys. This made things weird at rehearsal, because all of the songs were in keys like B, F-sharp and G-sharp. I learned to play in a lot of strange keys working with Duke, and I never did ask him why he played that way.

We used to rehearse songs for Harry and his artists in a small office with a tape recorder on Alexandrine off of Woodward in Downtown Detroit. When we made demos prior to going into the studio to record, we used the small bathroom in the back with the hard marble floors as an echo chamber for the voices.

Within a few months, the Royaltones signed a recording contract with Harry and Embee Productions. The company also hired us to do backup work in the recording studio for Del Shannon and its other acts. We were each paid five dollars to rehearse a song and fifteen dollars to record it in the studio. Harry would always tell us that our checks were in the mail and that we'd get our money in a week or ten days. Of course that never happened, so that became our running joke. Whenever anyone wanted to know how long something would take, we'd say "a week or ten days."

The Royaltones at that time consisted of George Katsakis on saxophone, Dave Sandy on saxophone and lead vocals, Bob Babbitt on bass, Marcus Terry on drums and me on guitar. I also wrote the arrangements. We had a kick-ass band in those days. In addition to the horns, we sang five-part harmony. Dave Sandy had a real high voice, and sang like Smokey Robinson on all the funky R&B hits, so he was our lead vocalist. For about three years, we packed them in wherever we performed in Metro Detroit. We also recorded quite a few singles. Our song "Our Faded Love" hit the national charts and was a huge local smash.

At the time when "Our Faded Love" was a hit, we were playing at the Dixie Bell bar on Vernor Avenue in Detroit. At the Dixie Bell, Bob Babbitt played trumpet as well as the bass. He would turn up the volume on his bass amplifier and play the bass with one hand by pressing the strings down real hard against the fingerboard while he played trumpet with his other hand. I never figured out why he started to play trumpet, but it sure gave our band a big fat sound.

One Friday night we were onstage at the Dixie Bell and the place was packed. George Katsakis decided to dedicate "Our Faded Love" to this girl we knew who was sitting in the audience. She was a pretty blonde, and when we started playing the song she got up and walked toward the bandstand.

Suddenly an empty beer bottle came flying through the air from her direction. George ducked as the bottle ricocheted off of Bob's trumpet, knocking the instrument out of his mouth. The bottle kept going and drilled the juke box dead center with a loud crash. We stopped playing. Bob was holding his lip. All at once, we looked at each other and started laughing. I guess the girl wasn't flattered by our dedication. The bouncer threw her out, and we never saw her again. I don't think we ever wanted to see her again.

George and Babbitt were always up to tricks. One night George tried to cut Bob's bass strings backstage with a pair of pliers. Of course, that was after Babbitt stuck a big wad of chewing gum under one of George's saxophone keypads and laughed while George honked and squeaked through an entire solo before he figured out what was wrong.

George retaliated during one of our famous high-stepping chore-ography numbers by moving off line and giving Babbitt a shove that sent him reeling off the stage into a table full of surprised customers. When Bob landed, his two-hundred-plus-pound body sent ashtrays and glasses flying all over the place.

As a member of the Royaltones, I learned to play a few tricks of my own. George used to sing lead to a few songs, using a high, squeaky voice like Frankie Valli's. One night we raised the key up a few steps without telling him, and he ended up singing so high and putting such a strain on his voice that I thought his vocal chords were going to explode. We all had a big laugh over that one—everyone but George. But he got over it.

Another time while we were recording at Golden World Studios, I wrote a bogus bass part of all thirty-second notes for Babbitt to play. There were so many notes on one sheet of paper that it looked like fly shit. When everyone was ready, I counted off the song for the band real fast. Once the band started, Babbitt began playing his part. He was in the corner of the studio huffing, puffing, and grunting with the strain. His face was contorted in intense concentration. Bob was beside himself, bouncing around in his seat trying to play those thirty-second notes. Suddenly things got out of hand and Bob fell backward and knocked a hole in the wall with the back of his head. He took it like a good sport, though because of his explosive personality I was never quite sure how he'd react.

In the sixties, Detroit was a rough and tumble, blue-collar, factory town. It was a common sight to see violence in the small bars that stood in the shadows of the dark, sinister automotive plants belching thick black smoke twenty-four hours a day. Men and women left the hot, stinking factories after working and sweating all day in the noise and blistering heat and headed for the bars at night to relieve their stress. Heaven help you if you got in their way or tried to push them around because after a few boilermakers to numb the pain they were cocked, loaded, and ready to fire.

Another bar we played in was called the Scenic Inn. The Scenic Inn wasn't very scenic, and it sure as hell didn't resemble an inn. One night on the bandstand, I heard wild screaming and yelling coming from the far corner of the bar. I looked over and saw a body flying through the air. There had been a fight, and the winner had lifted his opponent over his head and hurled him through a glass picture window and into the street. What a way to head home after a hard night of drinking and partying! The guy who'd been thrown out the window was so drunk that he probably never felt a thing. I'll bet he wasn't so fortunate the next day when he sobered up.

The Pullman Lounge was another fun spot we worked. The Pullman was on Schaffer Road in Dearborn. Why it was called the Pullman Lounge I don't know. There wasn't a train or a track anywhere in sight. The Pullman was as wild and disorderly as they came. If you caused any kind of disturbance at the Pullman, you bought yourself a whole world of trouble. If you were in a fight at the bar, the sadistic bouncers usually grabbed you by your hands and feet, lifted you up bodily, and made an end run for the front door. When they reached the door, they slammed your head into the knob a few times, like a battering ram, before you were launched out into the street like a ball shot out of an old rusty cannon. Phew! Another fine way to wrap up a hot summer night of dancing and entertainment!

I always made a point of staying up on the bandstand during these wild and woolly confrontations. If you entered the crowd during a fight, you were courting disaster. There was always the distinct possibility of severe personal bodily injury. I'm a lover, not a fighter, and I have five kids and two ex-wives to prove it.

One of the most interesting adventures in the life of the Royaltones happened at a bar on Fort Street in Lincoln Park called Harold's Club. Harold's Club featured a round piano bar facing an elevated stage. Most musicians are born show-offs, and although I'd started off my career with a bit of stage fright by now I was as bad as everyone else. The Royaltones were constantly looking for ways to delight, entertain, and amuse our audiences. We had records out and were well known in the area, so we got to perform live on the TV shows *Swingin' Time* with Robin Seymour and *Club 1270* with Lee Alan and Joel Sebastian.

After one show, we became friends with the TV technicians, and they showed us some pretty nifty special effects. One effect they had was called a flash box. The flash box was a metal electrical box with a switch and two bare wires separated inside the box. When you placed a charge of gunpowder in the box between the bare wires and pressed the electrical switch, the spark from the electrical current ignited the gunpowder, causing it to explode with a loud, brilliant flash accompanied by billows of puffy white smoke. At the time, we felt our audiences had become pretty blasé and jaded in response to our tricks and most of our current antics. After *Swingin' Time,* we ended up getting our own flash box from the guys at Channel 9.

Saturday night was a big night at Harold's Club, and this Saturday was no exception. That night we decided to bring the show to a climax with a big, loud bang. We loaded up the flash box with a charge of gunpowder and got ready for our big finale at the end of our fourth set. We were bouncing around onstage, playing our instruments like maniacs in a wild musical buildup leading to our big climax.

Toward the end of a wild, up-tempo rock & roll song, we pressed the switch to ignite the flash box. An earsplitting crash, accompanied by a huge cloud of white smoke and the biggest flash of light I've ever seen, shattered the noisy atmosphere of the club. The smell of gunpowder and burnt electricity brought tears to my eyes as it enveloped the stage and obliterated my view.

When the smoke on the bandstand finally thinned out, I saw empty barstools that had been occupied just a second ago by our loyal audience. The people who'd been sitting there had vanished, and it worried the hell out of me. A white mist hung in the air like an ugly supernatural fog. I walked to the edge of the stage and looked down. There they were. The force of the blast had apparently blown our entire audience out of their seats and down to the floor. The silence was eerie, but everyone got up and brushed off the white powder. When I saw no one was injured, I breathed a huge sigh of relief. Once they realized that they were OK, everyone commenced roaring and congratulating each other on their narrow escape from death. The fact that most of them were drunk on their asses probably made them more forgiving than they might otherwise have been.

At the end of the night, the band members came to the conclusion that in our exuberance and excitement for theatrics we must have placed too much gunpowder in our flash box, causing an explosion of far greater magnitude than we had intended. Today it would have been Lawsuit City. Fortunately back in the sixties people weren't so inclined to sue over anything and everything. But we learned two things from the incident—leave special effects to the experts who know how to use them properly and safely and find other ways to get additional audience response.

By 1963, when I first met Del Shannon, he'd already had monster hits with "Runaway" and "Hats Off To Larry" and had used the Beatles as an opening act when touring Europe and England. Whenever the members of the Royaltones and I recorded behind him, we would first rehearse the songs in Detroit and then record producer Harry Balk would fly us to New York. Our first recording took place at Bell Sound in midtown Manhattan.

When we arrived at the studio for our first session with Del, he needed an amplifier for his guitar. There were a few amplifiers already in the studio, but when Del asked to use one the recording engineer told him they belonged to the Manhattan Guitar Club, which included players like Kenny Burrell and Vinnie Bell. The engineer told Del that he would have to pay a fee to join the club before he could use the equipment.

That day Del was acting a bit like a prima donna until the music arranger, Bill Remel, put everything in perspective.

"Hey, Del," Bill said in his real loud New York accent, "why don't you play us a medley of your hit!"

Del grumbled but paid up, and then we recorded the first million seller I'd ever played on—a remake of a fifties song, "Handy Man."

After the session, Del treated me and the guys to a movie on Broadway. In those days, Times Square was pretty raw, with porno shows and two-bit hustlers on every street corner. I was still a young man, born and raised in Detroit, and when Del got ready to pay for the tickets he reached into his pocket, pulled out a gigantic wad of bills, nonchalantly peeled off a couple of fifties, and handed them to the ticket taker. I recoiled in shock.

"Del, are you crazy?" I nudged him with my arm. "It's after 3:00 A.M. in New York City on Times Square. Are you trying to get us killed? Put that wad of money back in your pocket," I said, "and let's get our asses inside before one of these hustlers decides to make you his next score."

Del just looked at me and laughed.

I worked with Del on many projects, including a big hit called "Little Town Flirt." The backup vocals were performed by a girl group from Detroit known as the Young Sisters. They had a record of their own that I had played on as well. At United Sound Studios in Detroit, Del and I even recorded a country album of Hank Williams songs.

In Detroit in the early sixties, it seemed that small independent record labels were popping up all over the place, like dandelions after a soft summer rain. Everyone in the country wanted part of the record sales action, and Detroit was no exception. I'm not sure why I started getting all those calls for sessions, but I think it was because I was one of the few guitar players in town who could sight read music, play tasty guitar fill-ins, and punch out hot solos.

I was playing on a lot of super record dates by now and recording hits with artists such as Little Carl Carlton ("Competition Ain't Nothin"), George Clinton ("I Wanna Testify"), and the Dramatics ("In The Rain" and "Whatcha See Is Whatcha Get"). Detroit was getting so hot that we recorded artists Paul Anka and Peaches & Herb in a studio garage called Pac 3, which was owned by recording engineer Richard Becker. The studio was located in a small, white garage behind Becker's house and had empty egg cartons on the walls of the control room and band room to trap and defuse the sound.

I remember standing next to Paul Anka in the studio. He was wearing a white Panama hat, smoking a small cigar, and looking very hip and continental. I looked at Paul and wondered to myself, can this be real? Are we so hot that artists would fly in from all over the country to record in a garage? The answer, quite simply, was a resounding yes. In the record business, when you're hot you're hot, and everyone wants to use you.

We cut "Good Night My Love," a hit for Paul Anka that day. On another day, we recorded the gigantic hit by the Floaters called "Float On" in the same garage studio. Every time we recorded a project for Columbia Records in the garage, they flew in their own engineer from New York to monitor the quality control of the recording process. I guess recording in a garage in Dearborn didn't exactly inspire confidence for the suits in charge of funding. Still, in those days, if you were from Detroit and had a product to sell or a project to record, major labels threw money at you.

Berry Gordy founded Motown just when the music scene in Detroit was really beginning to expand. The bars in the city were constantly jammed with paying customers, which allowed musicians to make a good living and practice their craft. In the beginning, Detroit bars were instrumental in giving many great bands their start. The Motown super pop group Rare Earth began as a bar band called the Sunliners, playing the Club Cliché on John R near Eight Mile Road in Detroit. Garth Hudson and other members of The Band played a mile over from Rose's Bar and the Dixie Belle at a place on Fort Street called the West Fort Tavern. In the fifties, I used to go to see rockabilly singer Jack Scott when he played at the Dance Ranch on Rochester Road. In the sixties, rocker Ted Nugent once let me borrow his stack of guitar amplifiers at a show we were both playing at the State Fair for political activist and poet John Sinclair.

Detroit also spawned many famous jazz and blues artists such as Kenny Burrell, John Lee Hooker, and Yusef Latef, who jammed in bars and small lounges all over the city. Members of the Motown rhythm section the Funk Brothers also got their start playing at clubs such as the Twenty Grand and Chit Chat Club. Even now, you can hear live entertainment in Detroit seven nights a week. The musical soul of the city lives on and transcends Motown, the record business, and any other influences to continue the city's rich musical legacy.

But things have changed a lot. As soon as they get good enough, many musicians now leave Detroit; they can't make a good living in the bars anymore unless they have a day job as well.

By the time Berry Gordy founded Motown, he had already scored hits as a songwriter, first in 1957 with "Reet Petite" and then with "Lonely Teardrops," both performed by Jackie Wilson. Less than two years after that first success, Gordy started his new company, initially known as the Tamla Record Company, on the back of an eight-hundred-dollar family loan. With their very first release, Marv Johnson's "Come to Me," the company had its first Top 30 pop hit.

In 1960, Motown moved into its new headquarters at 2648 West Grand Boulevard, and twelve months later they had their first number-one R&B hit with the Miracles' "Shop Around." And it was a Miracles album, *Hi, We're The Miracles*—along with *The Soulful Moods of Marvin Gaye*—that would be the first albums Motown released.

In late 1961, Motown had its first number-one pop hit, with the Marvelettes' "Please Mr. Postman." They came back in 1962 with "Do You Love Me?" by the Contours—at number three—and in 1963 with "Finger Tips Part Two," by Stevie Wonder, which reached number one. Berry's business savvy, along with his musical genius, had already proved to be an unbeatable combination. Every band I played with in those days was influenced by Motown's music and covered hits from the Temptations to the Supremes.

In 1964, Motown successfully competed with the "British Invasion" of the Beatles, the Rolling Stones, the Dave Clark Five, Herman's Hermits, and Petula Clark. They did it with three number-one hits by the Supremes, "Baby Love," "Come See about Me," and "Where Did Our Love Go?"; "Dancing in the Street," by Martha and the Vandellas, reached number two.

The following year, Motown had five number-one records: "Stop in the Name of Love," "I Hear a Symphony," and "Back in My Arms Again," by the Supremes; "I Can't Help Myself" by the Four Tops; and "My Girl," by the Temptations. Berry Gordy and Motown were burning up the charts.

In 1966, Motown had even more number-one records: "You Can't Hurry Love" and "You Keep Me Hanging On" by the Supremes and "I'll Be There" by the Four Tops. Berry and his powerhouse team of writer-producers, including Holland, Dozier and Holland, and Smokey Robinson, were succeeding in Detroit where so many others had failed.

At this time, I was still playing with the Royaltones, and whenever a new Motown record came out and went up the charts on the local radio stations we took it to our rehearsal and worked out the parts. I liked their funky sound, and as a musician I enjoyed their innovative chord changes. Never in my wildest dreams did I think I would ever get to play on one of these records. The people in Detroit loved Motown as well and went wild over their yearly Christmas Revues at the Fox Theater on Woodward Avenue.

Berry had redefined the rich musical heritage of Detroit and was beginning to make Motown and its artists known all over the world. But there was an entire musical scene happening in Detroit parallel to what was occurring at Motown. There seemed to be a storefront recording studio on every corner. In addition to working sessions at Pac 3, in 1965 I got my first call for a job at Golden World Studios. I was sitting at home one day taking care of my oldest daughter, Jordan, who was three at the time, when the telephone rang. It was Herman Weems, calling for Ed Wingate. He wanted to know if I could play a session for them.

The words *session* and *play* always caught my attention, so I perked right up. "When is it?" I asked.

"It started about an hour ago, and our guitar players are having trouble reading the music charts. Can you come on down and help us out?" he asked.

I told him I'd be there in about twenty minutes.

I hung up the receiver, loaded up my car with my guitar and special electronic effects, and put Jordan in the seat next to me. By this time, I was making enough money from playing music to have bought a brand new, bright red, GM Chevell. Things were definitely beginning to look up.

Herman Weems was waiting for me in the lobby, and he escorted me, with Jordan tagging along behind, into the recording studio, where the musicians were set up to record. I felt a little intimidated as I walked into the brightly lit recording studio for the first time and saw the rhythm section all set up and rehearsing tracks. It felt like I was walking into a crowded movie theater in the middle of a show and everyone was staring at me because I was late. I must have looked like some kind of musical hit man or hired gun brought in to handle a major problem. Once I sat down and looked around and saw the familiar faces of guitarists Don Davis and Eddie Willis, I felt a little more comfortable and relaxed.

Most recording studios I worked in were divided into two main rooms: the first was the control room, which contained the recording console, tape recorders, equalizers, and all the gear needed to record the music on tape; the control room was usually separated from the music room, or the tracking room, which was acoustically designed to reproduce sound as it is played.

The music room contained microphones, instrument amplifiers, and drum sets. This was where the musicians and singers did their thing. The record producer usually sat in the control room, which was separated by a soundproofed wall and glass window. He was assisted by a recording engineer, who also had an assistant to help place the various microphones in front of each instrument in such a way as to get the best possible sound.

At the time I was using a solid-body Fender Stratocaster because the Gibson Byrdland guitar I owned was too mellow and didn't have the right sound for R&B records. I got my guitar out of the case, sat down in the chair, and placed this little blonde toddler with blue eyes as big as half-dollars in the corner at my right elbow. She immediately stuck her thumb in her mouth while I studied the notes on the music stand. My fellow guitarists Don Davis and Eddie Willis were both smoking cigarettes and talking. I knew both of them were funky players and were good at reading chord symbols, but they didn't read much music notation or rhythms. As soon as I saw the chart, I understood why Herman Weems had called me. The music contained a guitar part that had to be played accurately with the bass and piano or the whole song fell apart. It was one of the main hooks of the song. I looked it over and told the music arranger I was ready. He counted off the song, I started playing the music, and they were back in business.

To someone who's never done it before, playing under such circumstances might seem simple. But to walk in cold and handle that type of situation took years of practice and preparation. You had to be clear-headed and calm and think fast on your feet. Being a studio musician is one of the most stressful jobs in music. The demands made upon you change each and every day. The stories of all that substance abuse in the studio have to be put in proper perspective.

If you were a studio player on call for sessions, you had to have your wits about you because you can't bullshit recording tape. Recording tape has no friends and never lies. When you're listening to the tape playback with the recording engineer and record producer, you'd better have played the right part at the right time or you won't be called back. In fact, you might even be sent home immediately and not get the chance to finish your first session.

The most difficult part of recording was learning how to play guitar lines and fill-ins that didn't interfere with or cover up the vocalist, even if they were overdubbed later on. To be a good studio player, you had to sight read music and play with the right feel and attitude to compliment both the artist and the song.

If you were in a self-contained band whose members always performed live when they were trashed, and your records sold well, you might get lucky and have a record company that didn't care how long you took in the studio—good luck! But if, on the other hand, a record producer had been given a time line and budget for his project, you'd better not be the reason he blew the schedule and went over budget.

In the studio, both the clock and the recording tape were always running, so every time you made a mistake the tape stopped and you had to do it all over again. If a producer didn't get all the songs completed on time, they had to pay the musicians overtime, which was super expensive. If they needed more than one hour of overtime, they might as well have done a double session because it would have cost them just as much.

At Golden World—and later at Motown—we usually recorded three or four songs a session, and a session lasted three hours. We never heard the song or saw the music before we walked into the studio each day. I remember getting paid overtime at Golden World, but I don't remember getting paid too much overtime at Motown. At Motown, they had it down to a science. Motown used the same basic musicians in the studio day after day, and as a result the musicians got very proficient at making great records.

I was feeling pretty good that day at Golden World Studios because Ed Wingate had a lot of money and I knew he did a lot of recording sessions for his artists on Ric-Tic Records. Ed had hits on Edwin Starr, the Reflections, the San Remo Strings, and J. J. Barnes to name just a few. Ed was clearly following in Berry Gordy's footsteps and was building a strong record label and stable of artists. I was glad to be onboard, but I didn't know what was ahead for Ed Wingate, Golden World Studios, and Ric-Tic Records.

Theo-Coff Productions

Working regularly at Golden World in the sixties was a great experience for me. I was a young musician trying to make a living playing music. The most money I could make in the clubs at the time was $200.00 to $250.00 a week for six nights. In the studio, I could make $60.00 for a three-hour session, so it didn't take me long to see where my future was.

It was at Golden World Studios that I met my future partner, Mike Theodore. Mike was younger than me and had the same type of intensity for the record business that I did. He originally played the drums in teen clubs and was now expanding into record arranging and production. I used to see him at the studio every so often. We met because guitarist Don Davis, who was also expanding into production, asked me if I could write some sweetening arrangements (violins) for a record he was producing on a young African American group called the Holidays. I wrote the arrangements, and because I was a student at Wayne State University and Don had a limited budget I hired some music students to play strings on the session. The session came out fine and the record, "I'll Love You Forever," was a moderate R&B hit. Because of that record, Mike Theodore approached me one day in the studio.

"I got an arranging job," he said. "It's for an artist, Steve Mancha, for Scepter Records, and it needs a full string and horn section. I can do the horns, but I've never written for violins, violas, or cellos. Maybe we could split the arranging fee and work together on this one."

"Sure," I said, "I can write for strings." After all, I thought to myself, I've already done it once—I'm almost an expert.

The next day Mike and I got together at his house on Montana in Highland Park, close to Woodward Avenue. We collaborated on the arrangements for rhythm, horns, and strings, which we wrote on a score pad as Mike played our parts on the piano. A musical score pad is a large pad with a separate staff for each instrument, so you can see what part is being played by each instrument throughout the song. It has enough lines for at least twelve instruments.

Mike and I approached arranging with pure gusto and enthusiasm, but in time we got a little jaded. Once we had access to large recording budgets, we looked up obscure instruments in a music dictionary, found someone who played one, and used it on a session for a new sound. We used everything from bagpipes to bass saxophones, bass clarinets, and bassoons, and we had fun doing it.

At United Sound Studios, near Wayne State University in Detroit, Mike and I conducted the session for which we'd made the arrangements. We recorded the rhythm tracks first. Then we came back and did the horns, followed by the strings. Our horn sections usually consisted of trumpets, trombones, and saxophones. We used a baritone saxophone or a bass trombone on the lowest part to add strength. In our string sections, we used violins and violas with cellos on the bottom. We didn't use a string bass on the bottom because we had an electric bass in the rhythm section.

Finally, we completed the Steve Mancha project successfully and moved on to other projects. Once we discovered how well we worked together, we formed a record production company. We combined both of our last names and called it Theo-Coff Productions. In addition to the projects we did at Golden World, we began to use a studio on Livernois in Detroit called Tera Shirma.

The first time I produced a record at Tera Shirma was in the early sixties. I had been called to do a few sessions, and one day Milan Bogden, the recording engineer, waved me over after we were done.

"Hey, Dennis," he called out. "Have you ever produced a record?"

"No, not really," I said, wondering why he'd asked.

"It should be pretty easy for a guy with your talent and ears," he said. "And I've got a group that needs to be produced. Why don't you give it a try? I think you'd be good at it."

Milan had sparked my curiosity, so I followed him into the control room, where he placed a tape on the four-track recording machine and asked me to listen to it.

As the music played, he moved to the beat and smiled.

"This is a new group we just signed," he explained. "I think they're good, but they need a little help to make their tracks really sizzle. There's something missing in their sound, but I can't seem to put my finger on it."

I listened to the tape and then went into the studio and added a few guitar parts. Then I remixed it from four-track tape down to two-track stereo. When Milan heard the new record, he looked at me and grinned.

"Yeah, man," he laughed. "That sounds a whole lot better. I knew you could do it."

"Well," I said, "as much time as I've spent playing guitar and arranging in the studio, I guess some of it had to rub off sooner or later."

I'm not implying that I was a great record producer, but as a musician I had worked with some of the greatest producers of the last two decades. Their names are legendary in the music business: Holland-Dozier-Holland, Norman Whitfield, Ashford & Simpson, and Stevie Wonder at Motown. I'd also worked with independent producers in Detroit such as George Clinton and Don Davis and West Coast producers Richard Perry and Quincy Jones.

One of the reasons why Mike and I got into record production full time was the deal we made with Tera Shirma Studios, which allowed us to go in at night and record local groups. If we signed any of the groups, we split the deal with the studio. Mike engineered, and I arranged and conducted the bands. I was playing guitar in a club band, so our sessions didn't start until about 3:00 or 4:00 A.M. The bands we recorded were also working clubs, so we all met at the studio after work to make music. The studio gave both of us keys, so we had no problem getting in after hours.

The first office we had for our new production company was a table in a go-go bar called Edjos on Woodward in Detroit. We used to come up with some of our best ideas while having a few beers and watching the girls. I don't know how that evolved, but I think we found the place kind of inspiring. Later we rented a real office, but it didn't have the same vibes, so occasionally we still conducted some of our brainstorming sessions at Edjos.

Tera Shirma was owned by two brothers, Ralph and Russ "Corky" Terrana, who were also musicians. Corky played guitar, and Ralph played keyboards. They were both part of the original group called the Sunliners, which eventually became Rare Earth. And it was with the Sunliners that Theo-Coff Productions finally hit pay dirt.

We had sent a demo of a record we made with the Sunliners to Clarence Avant in New York. Clarence was the president of the Maverick Record Company, which was distributed by MGM. Clarence listened to the tape and decided to sign the group to the label. He picked Mike and me to be the producers.

At the time, I was working with the Lyman Woodard Trio at the Frolic Showbar, and one night we were playing a funky instrumental version of the Isley Brothers' tune, "It's Your Thing." The crowd really went nuts over it. The next day I decided to take the trio into the studio and put it down on tape.

After I recorded the song, I sent a copy of the tape to Clarence Avant and another to Hank Cosby at Motown. Within a month, I heard from Clarence, who loved the record and signed me to a five-year recording contract.

Six weeks later, at Motown, Hank Cosby approached me at a session.

"Hey, Coffey," he said, "I played your tape for Berry. He really likes it and wants to sign you to a recording contract."

I had to tell him I'd already signed a contract with Clarence Avant at MGM.

Hank frowned, shook his head, and said, "Man, I sure wish you would have talked to me before you signed that contract. Berry really liked that record of yours!"

I had mixed feelings about signing with Motown. Even though I realized they certainly had the power to make me a star, musicians who worked in the rhythm section at Motown never had hits. I suspected that they were just too valuable in the studio backing up the company stable of artists and churning out the hits for Motown to really promote their records. Any success would have taken them out of the recording studio and put them on the road as headliners or an opening act. When I didn't hear from Hank, I assumed they weren't interested. The record business is the only business in which executives never tell you no; they usually just put up a wall of silence and refuse to answer your phone calls. As a record producer, I learned very early that in this business silence usually means no.

Maverick released an album on the Sunliners, but it didn't promote it well and the record flopped. Maverick then released one of my singles, "It's Your Thing," and it went up to number one in Detroit but didn't hit the charts nationally. Shortly afterward, MGM pulled the plug on Maverick, and my career and Theo-Coff Productions died in midstream, as everything came to a screeching halt.

After the lack of success of their first album, the Sunliners changed their name to Rare Earth and hired a new manager, who got them a deal at Motown. The new strategy paid off for Motown and Rare Earth because they recorded a live version of "Get Ready," which Mike and I had originally produced, became a tremendous hit. We had a contract with Rare Earth when they were the Sunliners, and Clarence Avant negotiated a small percentage of their royalties from Motown for us, so we did make a little money.

Mike and I now restarted our production company in earnest. One of the key ingredients in our survival was our investors, but many of them loved the music business without having a clue as to how it operates. We called them "Hokeys" because they were babes in the woods, and sometimes the music they wanted to record was very hokey or square. But if investors had the money we would record any song they wanted and make it sound professional. We were extremely customer focused.

One of the first investors Mike and I found was a big, burly Italian named John. John had written a few songs and wanted us to refine his melodies and record them featuring horns and strings. I remember quite vividly that day back in the sixties when we finalized our deal.

We were never quite sure about John's business, but we were all sitting at a table in my basement on Cavell Avenue in Livonia when John pulled out a large brown bag full of cash. He turned the bag upside down and dumped it on the table. We were both surprised to see twelve thousand dollars in cash neatly stacked in bundles of twenty- and fifty-dollar bills. John sorted the money and pushed it in our direction.

"Well, boys," he said, with a dangerous edge in his voice and a sinister look on his face, "here's the money to record my songs in the studio and pay the musicians. I'm sure you'll do a fantastic job." He moved in closer, invading our space just enough to make us uncomfortable. "But just so there's no misunderstanding between us . . ."

He reached under his shirt and pulled out a snub-nosed .38 revolver from the back of his belt and slammed it down on the table in front of us with a loud clunk. Mike and I were caught by surprise to say the least.

John, looking even more menacing, reached over and handed each of us a bullet.

"This time," he growled, "I'm handing you boys these bullets real nice. But if this record doesn't come out the way you say, the next time I give you a bullet you might not like my method of delivery. It could prove to be very hazardous to your health—capeesh?"

Mike and I nodded together in unison.

"Do we have an understanding?" John chuckled deep down in his throat.

"Sure, John, no problem," I finally managed to say, with a small tremor in my voice.

John got up from the table and walked up the basement stairs, leaving us mystified and a little apprehensive.

We swallowed hard, grinned weakly, and called after him. "Sure, John, you know we wouldn't screw you. Just wait till you hear it—you'll love it!"

After John left, I said to Mike, "He's joking right? I mean it's not like he's in the Mafia or something is he?"

Mike looked back at me, shrugged his shoulders, and said "How in the hell would I know? We just better make sure we do a good job and he likes the finished product."

The following week, we wrote the arrangements and hired the

musicians. One of them was our buddy Gordon Staples. Gordon was the concertmaster with the Detroit Symphony Orchestra, and he played an exquisite Stradivarius violin. Gordon played our arrangements and led the string section, and we recorded the songs. Then we mixed them down from the four-track to two-track stereo tape. When we were finished, we called John and invited him over to hear the finished product. This was to be the moment of truth; we felt we'd done a great job, but we weren't sure what John would think, and we were both more than a little nervous about the meeting.

We were sitting in my basement when I heard a car pull up to the curb and stop. I went upstairs just in time to see John get out of his brown Caddy and walk up the stairs to the front door. I let him in and escorted him to the basement. I noticed that he was wearing the same style of shirt, outside of his trousers, that he'd had on the last time, so I figured he still had his .38 revolver tucked in there somewhere. In spite of my apprehension, I played him the tape and the most amazing thing happened.

When John heard the lush arrangements of French horns and violins playing the melody—his melody—he was so moved that it brought tears to his eyes. Hearing the melodies that had been trapped inside his head expressed for the first time, he changed from a Mafia don type to a sentimental grandfather. Choking back his emotions, he looked at us through misty eyes.

"Boys," he said, as he waved his hand in a salute, "you really did a great job on my songs. I congratulate you on your artistry and talent, and I thank you from the very bottom of my heart!"

Mike and I looked at each other in shocked disbelief, but we quickly got ourselves together.

"Why, thank-you, John," I said. "Your songs are very beautiful, and it was a pleasure doing business with you."

Now that I think back on it, I wonder what would have happened if he hadn't liked them. Who knows? I wasn't wearing my bulletproof underwear at the time. Later I heard that John had got into an argument with someone at Tera Shirma Studios and had pulled his gun out and fired three bullets into the ceiling to make his point.

After the episode with John, I started getting more calls for recording sessions, especially since I'd begun recording for Ed

Wingate, the owner of Golden World Studios and Ric-Tic Records on Davison in Detroit.

Ed was a very large man who always wore gray business suits and carried a lot of money. He had the habit of handing out fifty-dollar bills to people and ordering them to go out for coffee or to run other errands. Ed always had plenty of the green stuff and didn't mind using it to get what he wanted. He really loved music but didn't fully comprehend the written musical notes and the arranging process, even though he knew what he wanted to hear.

Once, at the Uptown Theater in Philadelphia, Mike Theodore and I wrote some musical arrangements for a vocal group named the Fantastic Four. We hired local musicians to rehearse the charts so they could back the group in the show. The Uptown Theater had many rows of seats and was built like the Apollo Theater in New York.

During rehearsal, Ed kept walking over to the horn players and singing notes to them, waving his arms up and down to get their attention. Finally, the horn players got so ticked off that they stopped playing and just glared at Ed. If looks could kill, he would have been a dead duck right there on the stage. I finally intervened and called Ed over to the side. I explained that the horn parts were written on the charts and told him to be patient and let the guys read the music. Then he would hear the parts he wanted to hear. Ed piped down and didn't say another word, but the musicians still refused to play.

Ed was not a stupid man. He could read most people like a book, so he decided a peace gesture might be in order. He gave the musicians a break and then sent one of his gofers out to the liquor store to buy a huge Texas fifth of scotch, a bag of ice, and a package of plastic cups. When Ed presented his offering to the musicians, their mood lightened up considerably. They forgave Ed, and their of goodwill seemed to increase with each sip. After the musicians finished off most of the fifth, they resumed playing the horn parts. Later that night, the Fantastic Four sang in the show and the musicians performed just fine.

At Ed's Golden World Studios, I used to see Motown musicians Benny Benjamin, James Jamerson, and Eddie Willis moonlighting until they were caught and fined by Motown. Ed used Motown staffers on midnight sessions at Golden World and placed saxophonist Mike Terry and percussionist and tambourine player extraordinare Jack Ashford on weekly retainers.

Golden World Studios was professionally designed and equipped with all the latest in recording gear and audio technology. It had a high ceiling for string and horn overdubs along with an impressive recording console. The studio contained a brand new recording console that was even more impressive than the one at Hitsville, Motown's studio on Grand Boulevard.

When Ed sprinkled money over some of Motown's musicians in his rhythm section, and spread it around in marketing and record promotion, he was rewarded with his first big hit, "Romeo and Juliet," by a young white vocal group called the Reflections. Ed even hired New York arranger Tony Camillo to fly to Detroit, arrange the music, and conduct the studio rhythm section. That success helped to establish Golden World Studios and Ric-Tic Records as a new power to be reckoned with in Detroit. It was rumored in those days that if an independent record distributor refused to pay up he would be visited by a couple of evil looking guys in suits, with nicknames like "Killer" or "Big Tony," who would make them an offer they couldn't refuse. Ed always got his money.

When you examined the early success of Golden World Studios and Ric-Tic Records, it was amazing to see what money and power could accomplish in such a short period of time. Ironically, it was the use of money and power that got Ed into the music business and the use of it by Berry Gordy that eventually lured him out.

Prior to this, I'd been working in a band with singer Mickey Denton, but I started doing so many sessions later in 1966 that I ended up quitting the band and focusing on making records. Bob Babbitt played bass with me on most of those early sessions. Bob and I were constantly bumping in to each other at Detroit's many storefront studios. We would go into these little places in the back of a record store or in a former retail store and make records. After the session, we were paid in cash on the spot, and then we would go to the next studio. It seemed like anyone and everyone in Detroit was in the record business. I think the early success of Berry Gordy and Motown helped to drive it. In those early days, it was like a gold rush on the streets of Detroit. Some people struck it rich, but a lot of people spent a lot of money for nothing. At times, the streets of Detroit were littered with disappointments, empty wallets, and broken dreams. New record companies started up, and old companies disappeared. New studios were built, and old studios disappeared. Everyone wanted to get in on the action. You put your money up and built your recording studio and took your chances. No one ever said making hit records was easy, but a lot of great music was created in those days.

After a few years as record producers, Mike and I also became talent scouts for Theo-Coff and Clarence Avant. In addition to discovering Rare Earth, we discovered Jim Gold and the Gallery playing as a duo with two guitars in a small bar on Eight Mile Road on the east side of Detroit. We happened to stop by the bar one night because we'd seen that the place was jammed and we wanted to see what all the excitement was about. As we walked in the front door, I was amazed to see that the crowd was watching nothing more than two guys strumming acoustic guitars. One sang lead, and the other sang harmony. They didn't even have a drummer. They did use electric pickups to send the sound of their guitars through an amplifier, so the people jamming the dance floor must have been dancing to their guitar rhythms.

We walked up to the bandstand and introduced ourselves to the duo and to the lead singer-songwriter, Jim Gold. We told them we liked what we'd heard, and then we took them into the studio and recorded a demo tape, which we sent to Clarence Avant in L.A. We told Clarence that we wanted to sign the group to a contract, but initially he passed. A year later, when my hit single, "Scorpio," came out, we submitted the group to Clarence again. This time he took our word for it and signed them without even hearing them.

It was a good thing he did because we had three hits off their first album, "Nice To Be With You," "I Believe In Music," and "Big City Miss Ruth Ann." Singer Mac Davis wrote "I Believe In Music," and when he heard his song on the radio he called Jim Gold and pitched a bitch because he had left out the line "God loves you when you sing." I think Jim either forgot the line or singing the song in a bar every night made him feel funny singing about God. I know we thought he was singing the correct words at the time.

I still continued to do sessions at Golden World with artists such as Edwin Starr ("S.O.S.—Stop Her on Sight") and J. J. Barnes ("Real Humdinger"). One day, singer Bobby Goldsboro came in with a song he wrote for the Reflections. Bobby had us all in stitches because he kept making noises deep in his throat like a big old swamp bullfrog— Krebitchhh, Krebitchhh, Krebitchhh! The music business is the only business in the world, besides comedy, where you are encouraged and rewarded for acting crazy and bizarre. In music, all of your emotions lie just beneath the surface, waiting to burst out in some new combination of originality and creativity. In order to keep the creative process flowing, you sometimes have to be very childlike and uninhibited, give in to wild and explosive impulses, and hope they don't get you into trouble or arrested.

One hot day in July of 1967, we were at Tera Shirma Studios recording some rhythm tracks when suddenly the secretary ran into the studio and said a mob had just firebombed the drugstore down the street. She told us other buildings on the block were starting to burn and she was bugging out. Welcome to the Detroit Riots of 1967. I went over and looked out the front door, and sure enough the drugstore on the corner was burning and erupting with thick clouds of black smoke. I didn't see a mob of people at that time, but I knew the fire hadn't started by itself. Across the street, another building was just beginning to smolder and burn.

We all hurried back into the studio, leaving a lookout in case the flames moved too close. We started the tape machine and kicked out the jams, wanting to get the tracks recorded before the whole damn studio went up in flames. In Detroit, we always had both black and white musicians in our sessions, so at the time we didn't feel the riot as racial. In fact, we weren't really sure what the hell was going on, so we just completed our songs, grabbed the tapes, and got the hell out of there.

The entire city felt the impact of the riots, not least of all Motown Funk Brother, guitarist Eddie Willis, who was stopped in front of his own house by a tank. Eddie, who walks with a cane, told us the story later in the studio.

"Shit, I was driving home last night, and I see this tank coming right down the middle of my street. It stops right in front of my car, the turret swivels around, and some asshole sitting behind the turret points the damn cannon right at me.

"Hey, you," he yells down from the tank, "get out of your car with your hands in the air or we'll open fire!"

Eddie kind of shook his head with disgust and went on.

"I was scared shitless, so I got out of my car with one hand up in the air and my cane in my other hand, while the asshole in that damn tank asks me what I'm doing there. I got pissed and said, "What the hell do you think I'm doing here—I live here!'"

"Then a couple of soldiers came up behind the tank and pointed their rifles at me and asked to see some identification. After I flashed my driver's license to the soldiers, they let me go and told me not to go out after dark again this week because there was a curfew in effect for this area."

Eddie looked at me, frowned, and shook his head.

"Man, now how in the hell was I supposed to know that?!"

Later that week I was driving down Twelfth Street during the day, a few blocks away from the "blind pig" that had been busted, sparking the riots. I noticed that there was an armed National Guardsman standing on every corner. They were so young and looked like scared little kids. As I continued down Twelfth Street, I saw a guy hooking a motor from a burned-out car to a tow truck. Just then he was surrounded by three National Guardsmen with rifles. They pointed their rifles at the guy while one racked a bullet in the chamber with an ugly snap that made a lasting impression on me. I can't quite describe the feelings I had that day, but the sound of that rifle being racked was very ominous, so I kept on driving and minding my business. A few weeks later I began playing jazz with the Lyman Woodard Trio at the Frolic Showbar about two miles from that location.

In 1970, Mike Theodore and I signed up exclusively with Clarence Avant and his new label in California, called Sussex Records, which was distributed by Buddha Records. Both of us were now staff record producers, and I was signed up as an artist and a writer. The good part of this type of arrangement was the regular salary and the medical insurance. The bad part of a staff position was that when you finally arrived and started making hit records and all the major labels and big artists wanted to throw money at you to work with them on projects, you were stuck producing the acts signed to one label. Your chances for a hit were limited to a few artists, never the big superstars.

Well, it's all water under the bridge anyway. Life goes on. I'm just grateful that I had the chance to prove myself because the record business is filled with stories of people who never made it. That old phase, "It's better to have loved and lost than to never have loved at all," is the way I feel about my participation in the music business. At least I was engaged in all facets of the business.

In my career, I was a star and a success as a guitarist, arranger, producer, and writer. I did it all and then lost it all. But there's no sense crying over spilt milk. When it's time to move out, you're out—that's it. You really have no choice, but you still resist because the dream lives on. Once music gets into your blood, it never leaves. You're always trying to play your instrument or participate any way you can. I don't know why this is so, but it is.

Once Golden World Studios and Ric-Tic Records became successful and racked up some hits in the mid- to late sixties, Ed Wingate decided to get out of the business and sell it to—guess who? Berry Gordy—what a surprise! Berry did what American companies do all the time. He bought out the competition lock, stock, and barrel and signed the artists he wanted, like Edwin Starr. He made Golden World Studios part of his Motown empire. Motown producers still used Hitsville on Grand Boulevard for the rhythm tracks, but the high ceiling in the band room at Golden World made it ideal for string and horn overdubs.

When Golden World Studios became Motown and Ric-Tic Records was gone, other independent producers in town tried to pick up some of the slack, but Motown was now, more than ever, the biggest game in town.

DETROIT, 1968

The phone was ringing off the hook. I heard the noise pounding in my head like a persistent bill collector ringing the doorbell on the front porch. I cracked one eye open and felt the warmth of the early morning sun on my face as it radiated through the glass of my bedroom window. In the distance, I heard the roar of early morning traffic on the John C. Lodge Expressway. I tried to sit up and shake the sleep out of my head.

"Who the hell would call me this early in the morning?" I mumbled. I glanced at the clock on my nightstand and saw that it was nine o'clock. I definitely didn't feel like answering the phone this early in the morning. I'd worked late the night before playing guitar at Morey Baker's, the jazz club in Detroit, and I was still tired and worn out.

At that time, I was working at Morey's three nights a week with the Lyman Woodard Trio. The club had a long bar on one side of the room and tables and chairs on the other side. It also had a round, elevated stage about five feet above the floor against the far back wall. There was only enough room on the stage for about three musicians.

Morey Baker, the owner of the club, was a short, chubby Jewish man with pure white hair. Morey was a tough and experienced inner city bar owner who knew how to survive. He was a real social type and made friends easily. He mingled and partied with his guests. The club was located in an upscale neighborhood in Detroit and attracted high rollers and power brokers, including lawyers, judges, pimps, and gamblers. The parking lot at Morey's was filled each night with fancy Cadillacs and Lincoln Continentals.

The telephone kept ringing, so I finally threw back the heavy quilt I'd been sleeping under and sat up on the side of the bed. I made a mad grab for the telephone on the nightstand, just to shut it up. I brought the receiver to my ear and heard a familiar voice on the other end of the line.

Motown Calls
"The Rock & Roll Kid"

The brogue I heard on the other end of the line was unmistakable. "Wake up laddie, it's me, Jamerson. How ya doing?" The caller was Motown's legendary bass player, James Jamerson. I paused as I wondered why Jamerson was suddenly calling me. I had met him for the first time in a session we had recorded together a few months earlier.

"Fine, man, how you doing?" I answered. "What's going on?"

"I'd like to introduce you to someone. This is Hank Cosby."

The name Hank Cosby woke me right up. Hank was Stevie Wonder's producer and cowriter, and he was also one of Berry Gordy's right-hand men. As the music contractor who hired musicians to play on all of the recording sessions, Hank Cosby was a very powerful man at Motown.

"Coffey, how ya doing?" said Hank. "The reason we're calling is Motown's putting together a producer's workshop and we wonder if you'd be interested in playing guitar for us. It's going to be four nights a week upstairs at Motown Studio B, which is the old Golden World Studio on Davison."

"Sure, I'd be interested. Give me some more of the details?"

"We'll pay you $138.00 a week to work from seven to nine each night—Monday through Thursday—and Jamerson will be in charge. What do ya think?"

By now, I could hardly contain my excitement!

"It's next Monday," said Hank. "Let me put Jamerson back on the line. He'll fill you in."

Jamerson came back on the telephone.

"Hey, Coffey, since Motown put me in charge of this producer's workshop, there'll be me and you, Eddie Willis, Bongo, and some of the other Cats. It'll be cool, so come on down man."

I sat back down on the bed still wondering if I had heard what I thought I had. Just like that, without any warning, I had got a call from one of the most successful record companies in the world, and they had offered me a job. I had practiced eight hours a day since I was a kid for this moment, and now it was here! When you wait a long time for something to happen, and it finally happens, you still find it hard to believe.

My mind then flashed back to those live gigs I'd played with some of Motown's acts, such as the Velvelettes, the Marvelettes, and Edwin Starr. I was always trying to play my best to impress anyone from Motown, just so I'd be noticed.

I remembered an incident while playing with the Lyman Woodard Trio at the Frolic Show bar on the Lodge Service Drive.

One night, we were really kicking out the music in the middle of a set, and I looked up and saw David Ruffin, the lead singer from the Temptations, and Motown songstress Tammi Terrell walk into the bar together.

David was one of tallest people I'd ever seen. He looked like he was about six foot eight. They walked in and sat down at a table right in front of me. David, dressed in a brilliant white suit, was wearing an expensive gold watch and bracelet and those famous black, horn-rimmed glasses. Tammi was wearing a shimmering, white outfit and looked absolutely gorgeous.

The entire night, David and Tammi huddled together and seemed totally lost in each other. I was so impressed to see them in the club that I really tried to get them to notice my guitar playing. I knew a good word from David or Tammi would certainly help my chances of getting in at Motown. Melvin Davis, our drummer, was David's cousin. During the break, he introduced Lyman and me to Tammi and David.

Afterward I walked though the front door of the bar into the street to smoke a cigarette. Once I got outside, I couldn't believe my eyes. Parked right in the middle of the street was a shiny, brand spanking new Rolls Royce! You didn't see many of them in Detroit, at least not back then. The Rolls looked so rich and shiny, I halfway expected to see a chauffeur open the door and the Queen of England step out. I didn't see a driver or anyone else around. I wondered who was minding the store, because this neighborhood wasn't exactly Disneyland. Here I was, in the inner city after the '67 riots, playing in a bar for twenty dollars a night, and David Ruffin leaves a hundred thousand dollar car in the middle of the street unattended and goes into a bar with Tammi Terrell for a little music and entertainment. What a contrast in the lives of the "haves" and the "have nots." Suddenly I was face to face with the benefits of having really big money! I walked over and stared at the car in wonder. This was the first Rolls Royce I had ever seen up close. I peeked in the window. The interior was real varnished wood with seats of rich, polished leather, and I decided right then and there that I was going to work my ass off to get my part of the action. This was the effect Motown had on me. I knew Hitsville was the place to make money and play with one of the best recording bands in the world.

Monday finally rolled around, and at six o'clock I loaded up my car and drove down the Lodge Expressway. I got off at Livernois and continued down to Davison Street. I turned left on Davison, made a U-turn, and parked on the street in front of Motown's Studio B, a gray, two-story, cinder block building that used to be Golden World Studios. It was located about ten miles from Motown's Studio A.

Motown created the Producer's Workshop at Golden World to help evaluate their stable of in-house producers and to give them a chance to develop their ideas before going into the recording studio. I always felt that for some producers it was their last chance to come up with an idea for a hit record.

As I entered the building at Golden World to play guitar in the workshop, a uniformed guard behind a desk looked up and asked me to sign in. I wrote my name in the book and climbed the stairs on my right. At the top of the stairs, I entered a well-lit room and saw that James Jamerson was there and already set up.

Jamerson was an original character, with an attitude to match. He was about my height and weight, 5'10, 175 pounds, and sported a wicked Fu Manchu mustache. He could quite simply play the hell out of a bass. Jamerson and drummer Benny Benjamin really were the funky foundation of the Motown Sound. Jamerson played his fat, funky bass lines, and Benny pounded out the tight grooves and shuffles on his snare and high hat.

Jamerson usually wore black T-shirts, a black beret, Levis, and a brown leather belt with a small western buckle. Not only was Jamerson's bass playing extremely innovative, but his vocabulary had an interesting sound as well. As I walked in, Jamerson looked up at me and spoke in his Scottish-like brogue.

"Aye, me lad. What be-ith with you today?"

"Hey, man. Everything's all right. How's it going?"

"We ready to play the funk tonight Coff. You bring all your stuff?"

"You know me," I said. "I always come prepared." I got my wah-wah pedal and fuzz tone out.

Jamerson introduced me to the other workshop members: Ted Sheely on keyboards, Eddie Willis on guitar, Bongo Eddie on congas, and a new drummer called Spider. Ted Sheely was a quiet guy, a real gentleman, and very easy to work with. He just sat at the piano or electric keyboard, read the music, and played what he was asked to play. I never saw him much on the sessions at Hitsville, but I thought he could play very well. Of course, Motown already had Earl Van Dyke and Johnny Griffith, who were killer keyboard players.

Motown guitarist Eddie Willis was one of the funkiest guitar players out there. He always came up with real tasty ideas for every song. Most of the time he was given the freedom to play whatever he felt like because there were always other Motown guitarists on the session to read the music lines and guitar parts.

Eddie played a Gibson 335 hollow body guitar in the studio because the original Gibson Firebird he used at the workshop and on a lot of Motown sessions was broken. A Gibson Firebird was a thin, solid body guitar with a weird, obtuse shape. It had a sharp-edged sound that cut through an entire orchestra. (I knew this firsthand because I also owned a Firebird. Later, the nineties, I would lend it to the Henry Ford Museum for their Motown exhibit).

Eddie "Bongo" Brown was the funky groovemeister at the workshop and played percussion on most of the recording sessions I did at Motown. Eddie also played the fantastic conga solo during the percussion break on "Scorpio." Eddie originally hailed from Memphis, and he could really play those congas and bongos. Bongo didn't believe in reading music. I used to wonder why he was always grinning to himself while we were running down our parts in the song until one day I looked at his music stand during a session, and saw that he was reading a girlie magazine.

I remember a time in 1969 when I invited Bongo to a party at my house in the Detroit suburb of Farmington Hills. Although I was born and raised in Detroit, at the time I lived in the suburbs. My house was a two-story brick and aluminum home on a pie-shaped lot at the end of a cul-de-sac in a well-manicured subdivision.

I was standing in my living room having a drink with a few of the guests when I happened to glance out of my front picture window and saw a light green Volkswagen Bug go by. Five minutes later, I saw it go by again, and it finally dawned on me who it was: Bongo driving by my house for the second time. I ran out into the street, shouted at him, and tried to wave him in. He just kept right on going like he didn't even know I was there. I waited until he went by again, but this time I ran after him, waving and shouting even louder. Shit! I said to myself. I couldn't believe this guy was still driving right by me.

On the fourth time around, he finally saw me. He stopped in front of my house, and I ran over to his car.

"Man, what's wrong with you?" I shouted. "Didn't you see me waving?"

He leaned out of his car window and grinned sheepishly.

"Shit! Coffey, is that you? Damn, I thought you was some crazy white guy trying to run me out of his neighborhood."

It occurred to me that he probably felt as nervous in my neighborhood as I sometimes did when I went to see him in his. At

Motown, we were all colorblind, but other people in those days didn't see things that way.

Spider was the young drummer at the workshop. I don't know where he came from originally because he was quiet and never mentioned it. He played on a few sessions at Hitsville, notably the double-time drum cymbal part on "Cloud Nine." After that, he disappeared from the scene, and I really never heard where he went.

In the beginning, some of the producers came down to the workshop to try out their ideas. R. Dean Taylor was one producer who brought a few tunes to work on. He had one big hit with a song called "Indiana Wants Me," but after a few sessions he just faded from the scene. It may be that he left Motown. As a pop singer, he always had trouble getting Motown to promote him successfully.

The only successful pop R&B act Motown had was Rare Earth. They assigned ace producer Norman Whitfield to produce them and then broke them first on the R&B charts. I don't know why they had so much trouble promoting mainstream pop acts because most of their R&B acts crossed over to the pop charts anyway.

My biggest career opportunity began when Temptations' producer Norman Whitfield showed up. He used to come into the Twenty Grand in Detroit when I played there. Norman always wore expensive V-neck sweaters and fashionable dress slacks in the studio. He was very animated and explosive when he conducted the rhythm section. When Norman counted off each song, he would set both the tempo and the feel. Norman was a master of dynamics and built up each song to match what both he and cowriter Barrett Strong had in mind when they wrote it.

Once the Funk Brothers, Motown's studio band, got a good hold of a song in the studio, they played the hell out of it and added hot grooves and musical hooks galore. Like most Motown producers, Norman picked out which musical ideas he liked the best and recorded them in the song. A lot of producers at Motown, as well as producers at other major record companies, relied on the musicians to come up with good ideas to make hit records. But when the record became a hit everyone shared in the royalties except the musicians. In this, Motown was no different from anyone else.

Norman usually started the song off with the bass drum and percussion. Then he'd start adding instruments on each verse until the song built up to a crescendo of sweaty, raunchy funk! . . . and sweat we did. What I liked best about Norman was he always gave me the freedom to solo and experiment with my special guitar effects.

One day Norman came to the workshop with a song called "Cloud Nine." He wanted to experiment with the groove. Spider came up with a double-time cymbal part that resulted in a kick-ass groove, and I came up with the wah-wah pedal guitar effect in the introduction and throughout the song. When the pedal was pressed down and up, it produced a "wah-wah" sound on my guitar. The pedal had been used in pop rock by guitarists such as Jimi Hendrix and Eric Clapton, but no one had used it or even heard of it in mainstream R&B.

Even though some producers made use of the producer's workshop, activity there eventually slowed down. The producers lost interest and stopped showing up. Having nothing else to do, we just drank beer and watched stag movies every night. Well, what the hell—that was show business! Although the only big hit that came out of the workshop was "Cloud Nine," it happened to be the song that got me in the door at Motown.

A few days after we rehearsed "Cloud Nine," I got a call from Hank Cosby's office. They wanted me down at Hitsville the next morning.

The day of the session I was on pins and needles. I felt like I was getting ready for a concert appearance at the Philharmonic in New York. I could remember learning all the Motown records and playing them with the Royaltones in the local bars early on in my career.

As I drove up to the house on Grand Boulevard in Detroit and saw the sign, Hitsville, on the front, I suddenly realized that I too could become a part of the Motown Sound. I'd been packing them in at jazz and R&B clubs for the last two years, and I knew once they heard me play I'd be in like Flynn. Since I was fourteen, I'd been answering ads in the paper and auditioning to beat out other guitarists for jobs, and I had already played on hits with artists such as J. J. Barnes, Del Shannon, and Edwin Starr, so I was as ready as I'd ever be. I was a little nervous, but I was young and thought I could do anything. It never dawned on me just how many musicians got one chance at Motown and were never called back.

The actual recording studio was in the back of the house, but the main entrance was in the front. I walked up the steps and entered through the front door. A guard in uniform was sitting behind a desk. He asked me to sign in, so I wrote my name in the book and moved through the hall, past the control room, and went downstairs to the studio . . . the infamous "Snake Pit."

The room was well lit, and most of the musicians were already there. I could feel the energy and creative vibes flowing throughout the room, and for a brief minute I shook my head and thought to myself that this was the actual place where all the early Motown hits were recorded. I couldn't believe I was there. The place was awesome!

Growing up in Detroit as a musician, I had heard all sorts of Motown stories. A pop singer named Tommy Good signed a contract with Motown, and when his record wasn't released he actually had to picket Hitsville in front of local reporters to get his contract back. The industry standard contract in those days was a total of five years, with one-year options for renewal at the discretion of the record company. It was well known that Motown extended its contacts to seven years.

As I got ready for my first session at Motown, I looked around the Hitsville studio. It consisted of one long main room and two small overdub rooms with the guitarists all sitting together against the wall under the control room window. Jamerson was sitting on his stool next to the guitars, and both drummers were sitting behind sound baffles, or separators, against the far back wall. Later, in Los Angeles at MoWest, I would see the same sound baffles. Maybe Motown shipped them out from Detroit for luck, who knows? Bongo sat on the other side of the control room stairs, opposite the guitars. The electric keyboards and the tambourine were on the other side of him, with the acoustic piano and vibes located in the overdub rooms. The acoustic piano was sometimes placed in one of the overdub rooms to prevent the sound of the other instruments from leaking through the piano microphone and getting on tape.

The first person I spoke to was Jamerson, who was sitting on his stool smoking a cigarette. When he saw me, he looked over and grinned.

"Coffey, me lad, how be it with you? What's going on?"

I grinned back with my guitar in one hand and my special effects bag in the other. "Hey, man. I'm fine. Just tell me where I can set up."

Jamerson showed me how to plug my guitar into the direct box, which was connected to the big speaker they used for guitars. The guitars and his bass were routed directly into the recording console in the control room because there were no amplifiers. Motown gave us earphones and one big playback speaker so we could hear ourselves play. Jamerson took me around the room and introduced me to the musicians I didn't know. Everyone was smiling and real friendly, so I felt right at home.

My guitar was a Gibson Firebird that had I bought after hearing Eddie Willis use one on a recording session we did together. I really liked the sound of it—a good, tight, funky sound. I had also brought the leather bag that contained my special guitar effects. The only effects I had at the time were a fuzz tone (a distortion device) and the wah-wah pedal.

Once I got my gear set up, I looked at the music chart sitting on the stand in front of me. I saw that the notes were written on a double staff just like piano sheet music. The guitar figure and bass figure were written in sixteenth notes.

I soon learned that we were expected to record one song per hour—no small feat. We had to sight read a new chart every hour, improvise guitar fills or a solo, and try to make a hit record all at the same time. Each session lasted about three hours. On most days, we did double sessions with an hour off for lunch. We usually went to lunch at the Howard Johnson's restaurant on Grand Boulevard just down the street.

Later, I would discover that we'd been recording six songs a day, five days a week. The number of hits we made was astonishing! They didn't call Motown the hit factory for nothing. I used to collect all the records I played on, but after a while there were just so many that I couldn't keep track of them. I played on at least one hundred million sellers for Motown and the other companies that used me. At one point, I was on three of the Top 10 and ten of the Top 100 singles on the *Billboard* chart every month for an entire year.

That day on the session we had two drummers. Spider played high hat and cymbals, and Pistol Allen played snare drum and foot pedal. Most people didn't realize it, but the concept of using two drummers was born on that session. We used two drummers on almost every session after that. That was how the drum cymbal parts on Motown records became so rhythmically complicated. I was sure that a lot of drummers working in bars and clubs were going crazy trying to duplicate the drum sound of Motown by attempting to play both drum parts at once.

The rhythm section I usually played with at Motown consisted of Earl Van Dyke and Johnny Griffith on keyboards, Eddie "Bongo" Brown on congas and bongos, and James Jamerson on bass. There was also Jack Ashford on tambourine, Jack Brokenshaw on vibes, Richard "Pistol" Allen and Uriel Jones on drums, and Joe Messina, Eddie Willis, or Robert White on guitars. Usually there were three of us playing guitars at each session, but some sessions had as many as four guitars. All of the guitar players at Motown, including me, cooperated with each other to make things easier. No one tried to hog the best guitar parts or tried to take over, like I later saw in L.A. and New York.

At Motown, we all worked together to make the best records we could. I played with other musicians at Motown, including bassist Bob Babbitt and drummer Andrew Smith, but I worked with these musicians the most. The arrangers I worked with the most were Paul Riser, Johnny Allen, Dave Van Depitte, and Wade Marcus.

I learned that the song we were to record on my first day at Motown was "Cloud Nine." Now I knew why they'd called me for the session. Norman had obviously liked what I'd done at the workshop and finally wanted to use me on a record date. Sometimes all it takes in the music business is one big break. This was the break I'd been waiting for.

Norman counted off the tempo, and everyone started playing. I ad-libbed a fast wah-wah effect in the introduction and played the written figure on the guitar through the wah-wah pedal. It immediately became very clear to me that I was playing with the finest rhythm section I'd ever heard.

Once I learned the song, I began to listen more closely to what the other musicians were playing and to the interaction going on between them. Each musician complimented what the other musicians were doing. When one guy locked into a musical idea, the others supported it and built new ideas on it. Music is one of the truest expressions in the human experience. It comes from deep within the soul and communicates feelings and passion to the listener and can also stimulate the imagination to recall meaningful past relationships and events.

On the last verse of the song, the groove we were playing was so hot that I just had to jump in and play a solo. I cranked my volume up a bit, closed my eyes, and let 'er rip. It didn't get much better than this. I was finally playing at Motown's Hitsville studios with the finest damn band in the world and getting paid good money for it too. The rhythm section was so funky and exciting that I couldn't help but play a great solo. I gave Mr. Wah Wah Pedal a hell of a work out that day!

The sound of Motown on the radio was always fantastic, but to be playing guitar right in the middle of it in the studio was unbelievable! I never forgot the excitement I felt the first time I played for Motown, which to me was like a baseball player getting his first shot in the major leagues. I hit a home run my first time at bat with "Cloud Nine," which went on to become an international hit for the Temptations. The success assured me a regular slot on the home team. I was now a guitarist, and the effects specialist, at Motown.

Cloud Nine and All Points South

After my first session with Motown, I was so excited I felt like I was on cloud nine. It just didn't get any better than this! The Motown workshop I was in four nights a week, led by James Jamerson, remained quiet due to the lack of interest of Motown record producers. Motown had already got rid of its staff producers who were hitless, so the remaining producers continued to develop their ideas during the sessions themselves. I was now beginning to get calls to do sessions at Motown five days a week. We usually started at 11:00 A.M., played one session until 2:00 P.M., then broke for lunch and came back and did another session from 3:00 to 6:00.

When the Motown Producer's Workshop was still happening and busy, I'd complete two sessions at Motown, eat dinner from 6:00 to 6:30, and play guitar at the workshop from 7:00 to 9:30. Then I'd begin a session at 10:00 at Tower Studios on Grand River in Detroit for Holland-Dozier-Holland (HDH). Holland, Dozier, and Holland were the ace songwriting and production team responsible for most of the early Motown hits for the Supremes and the Four Tops. They were superstars in their own right and lived as high off the hog as any Motown recording artist—maybe even higher.

At Motown, HDH had created such hits as "You Can't Hurry Love," "You Keep Me Hanging On," "Love Is Like An Itching In My Heart," and "Baby Love" by the Supremes. They also produced

"Reach Out, I'll Be There," "Bernadette," "It's The Same Old Song," "Shake Me, Wake Me When It's Over," by The Four Tops; "Heat Wave" and "Nowhere To Run," by Martha & the Vandellas; and "How Sweet It Is" and "I'm A Road Runner," by Junior Walker. Considering the number of hits HDH gave Motown, they should have been given a senior partnership in the company.

Brian Holland was an urbane, articulate man—a pipe smoker with a Van Dyke goatee. Along with Lamont Dozier, he worked with us in the studio and conducted the rhythm section. With that pipe in his mouth, Brian looked like he could have been hanging out with Hugh Hefner at the Playboy Mansion. Lamont bounced around in the studio with a lot of energy, in contrast to Brian, who was very laid back. Eddie Holland was similar in character to his brother Brian, but he usually stayed behind the board in the control room with the recording engineer when we recorded the rhythm tracks. Eddie used to be a lead singer at Motown and once had a big hit record called "Jamie." I assumed his expertise in the studio was working with the singers and recording engineer.

The most interesting thing about working with this extraordinary team of record producers and songwriters was the way they separated their musical arrangements into three parts, identified by letters A, B, and C. Letter A was the verse of the song, letter B was the chorus or hook, and letter C was the bridge. Sometimes they used letter D at the end of the song to identify the vamp or fade. When we played the arrangements in the studio, HDH would constantly switch the sequence of each section until they felt the song sounded right. Then they'd nod, grin at each other, and say, "OK—that's it, let's cut it!" They were creating the final sequences of the arrangement using gut instinct and experience, but I also think they were waiting to see what musical ideas and grooves we came up with for each section of the tune.

In the latter part of the sixties, HDH became disillusioned with Motown and defected to start two record companies of their own, Hot Wax, which was distributed by Buddha, and Invictus, which was distributed by Capitol.

I recorded many hits for HDH on their own record labels, including "She's Just Another Woman," by the Eighth Day; "Give

Me Just A Little More Time," by the Chairmen of the Board; and "Mind, Body and Soul," by the Flaming Embers. I also recorded "Band Of Gold," by Freda Payne, and "Want Ads," by the Honey Cone. At the time, HDH was going through a big legal battle with Motown, but they still had the magic touch in the recording studio.

Holland-Dozier-Holland built a new recording studio in the back of the old Tower Theater, where as a child I had gone on Saturday afternoons to watch movie matinees. Their studio setup was a little different because their offices were in the front of the theater by the lobby while the projection booth was made into a control room. The actual music studio was in a room built on the stage. Another friend of mine, Artie Fields, who was in the car jingle and commercial business, built the same kind of studio on Woodward Avenue by Clairmont in Detroit.

Although HDH had many hit records, eventually things deteriorated and they had to close both of their record companies. The rumor was that they had tried to operate their companies and spend money like Motown but didn't have enough capital to support that amount of overhead. Perhaps if they had started smaller they would have survived—but who really knows?

As busy as I was recording for Motown and HDH, one day I received a telephone call from Brad Shapiro and Dave Crawford, the record producers for Wilson Pickett. Brad offered to pay me double scale and all expenses if I'd fly down to Muscle Shoals, Alabama, and spend four days recording Pickett's new album.

The week of the session, I boarded a small prop plane and flew into the tiny airport in Muscle Shoals. Muscle Shoals was a small, sleepy, southern town next to the shoals of the Tennessee River. It was a dry county, where you could get into serious trouble with the police or the county sheriff for having an empty beer can in your car.

When I got off the plane at the airport, Brad, Pickett, and Dave met me in a rented car and we drove to the Muscle Shoals Sound recording studio. The studio was in a long, gray, cinder block building that looked like anything but a recording studio. It was amazing to me that here, in this small, out of the way town, there were actually two famous recording studios, Muscle Shoals Sound and Rick Hall's Fame Studios.

The musicians who collectively owned Muscle Shoals Sound used to work for Rick Hall, but they had a falling out and left Rick to buy their own studio. It was an interesting phenomenon that major stars like Bob Seger, the Osmond Brothers, and even the Rolling Stones came to Muscle Shoals to record. I guess what's true now was true then: if you're good, everyone beats a path to your door, no matter how far off the beaten path it is.

The pace at Muscle Shoals was very different from the pace at Motown and other studios up north. At Muscle Shoals, we usually finished one song every three hours, compared to one song per hour at Motown. This was quite a difference in time, but the musicians also owned the recording studio, so they made additional money in studio time. The laid-back Muscle Shoals recording strategy was so successful, and produced so many hit records, that the musicians actually demanded and received 1 percent of retail record sales in royalties from the record companies.

"Don't Knock My Love," the first song we recorded for Pickett, was a huge success. I brought down all my toys and doubled the bass line with a special guitar unit called the Condor. The Condor was built by the Hammond Organ Company and consisted of a guitar and a keyboardlike device, which allowed you to push in stops and create sounds for the guitar, such as an organ, harpsichord, bass, and bassoon. I also used the Condor for my solo on the hit record "Smiling Faces" by the Motown group Undisputed Truth.

With all of the new acoustic studio designs and fancy recording rooms, I was surprised that two of the most successful recording studios I have ever worked in were square or oblong rooms with bare walls. Hitsville and Muscle Shoals Sound didn't have the wild and exotic wall surfaces and curves that expensive recording studios of today use to trap or reflect different sound waves. What they did have was experienced rhythm sections that consistently created hit records, year after year.

The session at Muscle Shoals Sound usually began with Barry Beckett, the piano player, listening to a demo of the song and writing out the chords. Then Barry would write out the chords on a sheet of paper, using the Nashville Numbering System. In Nashville, where they don't use written music, they use a numbering system to give the musicians the chords and arrangements for each song.

The Muscle Shoals players were Barry Beckett on piano, Jimmy Johnson on guitar, David Hood on bass, and Roger Hawkins on drums. They had played with Pickett before and were all nice guys and excellent studio players. When the big crunch hit the record business in the early eighties, Muscle Shoals got cold, just like Detroit, so some of the musicians moved up to Nashville. Barry Beckett is now a very successful country record producer who has worked with artists such as Hank Williams Jr. and Confederate Railroad.

The following year, Brad called me to do Wilson Pickett's next album. This time Brad and Dave decided to record Pickett at RCA studios on Music Row in Nashville. In Nashville, I played with a guitarist by the name of Reggie Young, who recorded with Elvis and other artists at American Studios in Memphis. When American Studios closed in Memphis, Reggie moved up to Nashville, where he still plays today.

The next time Brad called, he offered me a session at Criteria Studios in Miami to make an album for Jackie Moore, an Atlantic artist who'd just had a big hit with "Precious, Precious." This time I brought along some of the Motown Cats, including guitarist Eddie Willis, percussionist Jack Ashford, and Rare Earth guitarist Ray Monette. When we arrived at the studio, Jerry Wexler, the legendary producer, and founder and co-owner of Atlantic/Atco records, greeted us warmly. Jerry was a super nice guy, who often joked that he was probably the oldest record producer still in the business. He also let us use his cabin cruiser to go fishing all day in the ocean. He told his captain not to come back until we caught some fish. We had a lot of fun that day and caught plenty of fish, including a massive barracuda I pulled in.

The day before I left to come home, Jerry offered me a staff job in Miami for Atlantic Records. Because Miami was still a small operation, he offered me thirty thousand dollars a year to be on call for Atlantic. Unlike the situation at Motown, I could work for anyone else in my free time. I had to turn him down because I was already making more than twice that in Detroit.

We had a real ball in Miami working on the session. One of the staff musicians for Atlantic was Dr. John, the wild and crazy keyboard player and singer from New Orleans. He played with a lot of soul, not to mention his far-out New Orleans accent. Dr. John always stands out in a crowd, and you can hear evidence of his unique vocal style on his hit song, "Right Place Wrong Time."

After one of the sessions, Ray Monette and I stopped by Dr. John's apartment for a visit, during which John brought out some of his stash and we all had a little toke. Grass had never been my thing, but since the other guys were doing it I thought I'd give it another try. Man, that shit was as strong as hell.

We said goodbye to Dr. John, left the apartment, and began walking back to the recording studio. We wandered down the street in a deep mental funk, feeling the effects of the grass. We couldn't figure out where in the hell we were or how to get back to the studio, even though Dr. John's apartment was just a block away. We drifted aimlessly up and down the street, enjoying the warm night air. After awhile, we became a little concerned because we still couldn't find the studio.

Finally we looked up, and the studio appeared from out of our funk. We opened the door and stumbled in. I had no idea what time it was, but I know we must have been wandering around for quite a while. I don't smoke anything anymore, not even cigarettes, because all that stuff is hazardous to your health.

Live in the Motor City

In 1968, I was still playing guitar at night with the Lyman Woodard Trio at Morey Baker's. I had a lot of fun there, and we were still packing them in. We stayed at Morey's for about two years. Motown record producer Norman Whitfield and his prodigy Clay McMurray came in to hear us play some nights. Norman was producing Marvin Gaye, the Temptations, and Gladys Knight, and Clay was producing Gladys Knight and the Originals. I even met vocalist and TV star Della Reese and her manager, who were sitting at the bar one night. Morey's was the "in" place to go and stayed jammed with people every week, Thursday through Sunday. Today I still bump into people who used to go there and fondly remember it. In fact, when I sat in at Emanual Steward's place in Downtown Detroit in August of 1994, a man came up to me after the set.

"I knew that was you playing," he said. "And when they announced your name over the microphone I was sure of it. I live in Minneapolis now, but I used to see you play at Morey Baker's all the time. You still sound great, and I enjoyed hearing you play again."

I was flattered that he still remembered me. He wished me luck and walked away. I was glad to still be around and able to play guitar after all of these years.

I had one routine I used to do at Morey's that brought the house down. When the groove was happening on any hot tune each night, I used to turn out all of the stage lights by stepping on a foot switch, which also activated a strobe light. The strobe splashed the entire band with weird lighting and flickering psychedelic images. The people in the audience had never seen anything like it before. They clapped like mad every time we did it.

In the late sixties, I went from playing at Morey Baker's to opening the show for the Temptations at Cobo Hall in front of an audience of fifteen thousand people. That was a real change for me, and it took a lot of energy and effort on my part to get used to it. In the past, I'd always enjoyed the intimacy and surroundings of small jazz clubs, where I could see and talk to the audience face to face. In a huge concert arena, the only things I saw were bright lights and rows of seats that seemed to go on forever until they finally disappeared into the vast darkness high above the stage. I figured this was what stardom was like and that I'd better get used to it if I wanted to continue in the music business.

It was also around this time that I really came to understand some of the more unsavory aspects of the business. Guys like Earl Van Dyke and Jamerson, who were company men, were beginning to wonder where the big profits were going from all those million-selling hit records they recorded day after day. They could see that the really big money was passing them by. If they bitched too much, Motown and Berry would give them a writer's advance or something else to shut them up. I never heard the whole story about the confrontations between Motown management and the musicians over money, but I heard enough to know that they were beginning to feel used and underpaid.

In addition to being underpaid at Motown, they had the problem of being contractually prohibited from playing for anyone else—a prohibition Motown strongly enforced. I recall one Sunday morning at 4:00 A.M. when I was playing on a non-Motown recording session at United Sound Studios in Detroit. This was before I worked at Motown. James Jamerson and Eddie Willis were also playing on the session. Suddenly there was a loud banging at the back door. After the banging stopped, the door flew open and I was surprised to see one of Motown's "hatchet men," attorney Ralph Selzer, standing there wearing a dark trench coat. Ralph really didn't have to say anything. He just pointed his finger at Eddie and Jamerson and smiled. He then turned around and vanished back into the night like a ghostly apparition. It was still dark outside.

"Shit," Eddie mumbled under his breath.

Jamerson just shrugged his shoulders and began playing. Motown fined them five hundred dollars each for attempting to earn a little extra cash on an outside session.

When Jamerson told me about the fine, I said to myself, "This is absolutely ridiculous. Motown sends their spies out at 4:00 A.M. on a Sunday morning to catch their guys playing for someone else. Is this even legal? What about the rules of free trade and fair competition?"

Motown deliberately denied the musicians credit on their albums to keep their identities secret. In fact, Valerie Simpson, of Ashford & Simpson, was the first producer-writer who insisted that we get credits on an album we recorded for her on a Motown artist. She also gave me credit for a guitar solo I performed on the record. She knew it was important for a musician to receive album credits because it resulted in additional work opportunities. Valerie told me it was done routinely in New York City, where she lived, and should be done in Detroit too.

In the sixties and early seventies, Berry Gordy and Motown maintained a stranglehold on the musicians and their creativity. Berry followed the Golden Rule—"He who has the gold, rules." Motown successfully kept the members of its house band, the Funk Brothers, from recording for anyone else, which is one of the main reasons why the Motown sound was copied but never equaled.

Of course, that was before Motown moved to Los Angeles in 1973. After that, it was every man for himself.

Despite these problems, the day-to-day sessions at the Hitsville studios continued as before. We were still making great music and still having a lot of fun. In particular, I remember a session with two female record producers from L.A. who were in Detroit to record some tracks for the Supremes. These girls were breathtaking in their tight cutoffs and California T-shirts. One girl was a voluptuous blonde bombshell, and the other was a foxy African American princess. Both of these girls immediately caused the Cats to do some "California Dreaming" and probably brought to mind a lot of other visions as well.

I think these fine ladies miscalculated the music scene in Detroit. When I lived in L.A., it was perfectly acceptable to bring out the treats in the recording studio. Producers would sometimes provide alcohol, drugs, and snacks to the musicians during a session. But in Detroit providing the musicians with goodies could be a serious mistake. The producers had a table positioned in the hallway before the door that led down the stairs into the studio. The table was covered with a nice white tablecloth. On the tablecloth was a fabulous offering of whisky, scotch, beer, pop, a bowl of fresh fruit, and a plate of fancy cheeses.

When the Cats arrived for the session, things began to go downhill. Most of the Cats played music in the local clubs, and as a matter of courtesy they never refused a free libation when one was offered—especially by two fine ladies.

During the session, the Cats started drinking and getting hammered. Next thing you know they were asking the girls to check out the music, saying they saw a mistake on the chart. Of course, this was just a ruse to try to cop a little feel. Every time one of the girls tried to count off a song or conduct the session, someone would make a remark to get her attention.

"Hey baby" they'd yell, "I need some help with my part! Why don't you come a little closer to me, I can't hear you from there."

Things got so far out of control that the girls fled the session without even getting one good take. At least their virtue remained intact, if just barely.

I was surprised when I saw the same two producers back for a repeat performance the following day. They were ready to record, but what a difference! The girls had so many clothes on there wasn't a bare patch of skin to be seen anywhere. Each girl was covered all the way up to her pretty neck and had her hair tied back in a severe bun like a spinster elementary school teacher. There were no legs or cleavage, no nothing. The girls didn't smile at the musicians or offer any treats, and it was strictly business from then on. I think the rest of the Cats felt sorry for the girls, so we were on our best behavior that day. We played their music with the appropriate creativity and enthusiasm and gave the girls some good rhythm tracks to take back to California.

Another day at Hitsville we were recording the Spinners' tune

"It's a Shame," and Stevie Wonder was making his first appearance as a record producer. Stevie had an ear for music like no other producer I've ever worked for. Nothing got by Stevie. He could be difficult to work for because he often sang the exact part he wanted played, right down to the phrasing, or execution of each note. I always felt a little stifled working with him, because he would dictate the part he wanted so precisely that it was often difficult to concentrate on what you were playing—you were too busy trying to remember how he wanted you to phrase each note.

That day in the studio he was in rare form. In addition to being an excellent singer, writer, and keyboard player, Stevie was also a terrific drummer. The two regular Motown drummers were also excellent players; under any conditions, they could kick out the jams and play. No one knew this better than Stevie since many of his hits had been recorded with the Motown drummers.

At this time, Stevie was clearly beginning to march to the beat of a different drummer—different from the slick, urban sound Motown Records and Berry Gordy had marketed so successfully in the past. On that day, Stevie was demonstrating to all of us just how different he was going to be. The Cats and I began playing the arrangements as written and trying to find a good, funky feel for the tune. Usually, the Motown musical arrangements were well written, but we added our own ideas to really make the music and songs come alive. The feel and intensity we all put into the music at Motown transcended any mere notes written on paper. The musicians at Motown used the music arrangements as a road map. The map showed us were we were headed and how to get there, but it didn't tell us which method of transportation to take. We decided that along the way.

After rehearsing the arrangements, Stevie walked over to Pistol Allen and Uriel Jones, the two drummers on the set, and sang the drum part that he wanted one of them to play. Uriel and Pistol could play anything, and probably have at one time or another, but Stevie was insistent and wouldn't give up until they played the part exactly as he envisioned it. Finally, after about fifteen minutes of exasperation, both of the Cats got up off their drum stools.

"Shit, man," Pistol said in exasperation, "if that's what you want, you sit down here and play it because we just don't feel it that way!"

Stevie sat down behind the drums and did just that. He played what he heard in his head, what the other drummers couldn't hear. I don't recall the drum part being that radical, but it was different. Stevie played the drums on the session, and we completed the tracks to his satisfaction. I guess he proved himself as a producer that day because "It's A Shame" by the Spinners was a huge success.

From that point on, Stevie kept trying to break the mold at Motown. I heard he almost left the company over the right to compose and produce his own music. Eventually Berry Gordy and Motown must have wisely relented, because Stevie remained with Motown when a lot of the other artists were going their separate ways. I don't think the artists who left Motown, or the Motown that left Detroit, ever did as well or had as major an impact on the sound of American music as they did when they were here in Detroit. The Motown Sound created at Hitsville in Detroit was widely imitated but never really duplicated.

Stevie never used the Motown Cats much after that. He made some great-sounding records, but they didn't resemble anything recorded at Hitsville on the Boulevard in Detroit, so more power to him. He invited all the Cats to the wedding reception at the Mauna Loa restaurant on Grand Boulevard celebrating his first marriage. I thought it was a pretty wild affair, with some of the Cats providing the music.

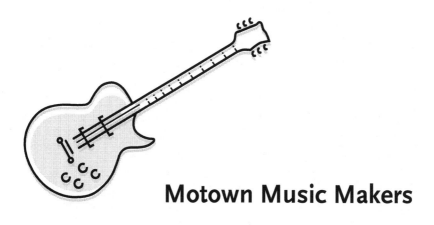

Motown Music Makers

If the members of the Motown band had stayed together after the company left Detroit, things might have turned out differently. But unfortunately the major record companies had not built offices or studios in Detroit because they knew they couldn't get the musicians. One by one, the musicians left town to seek work. A few stayed in Detroit or eventually drifted back after living on the road. Keyboard player Earl Van Dyke told me that after he came off the road with singer Freda Payne he found a position as artist-in-residence at a high school in Detroit. At the time, most of those positions paid four hundred dollars per week plus medical coverage. Earl was one of the more fortunate ones—at least he had steady work. He helped make millions for Motown, and this was his reward—playing with a trio at night and working at a high school.

Earl was the Motown bandleader and godfather of all the musicians. He was a large, chunky man, who had a master's degree in music from a college in New York City. He was the consummate musician's musician. He usually had a goatee and wore polo shirts and dress slacks on the sessions. He was the most responsible man in the band, in contrast to drummer Benny Benjamin and bassist James Jamerson, who sometimes acted out with wild and erratic behavior. Earl was also the leader of a band made up of Motown musicians Robert White, Uriel Jones, and James Jamerson, which played four nights a week at a funky little place on Twelfth Street in Detroit called the Chit Chat Club. The fact that some members of the Funk Brothers played together regularly helped the studio band develop more continuity and cohesiveness as a unit.

Earl always drove a shiny, black, Fleetwood Brougham to the sessions. The car matched his personality and position in life, as Motown's bandleader and top piano player. Earl always acted like a professional musician and was an intrinsic part of the Motown sound. The last time I used Earl in the recording studio was on my album *Motor City Magic,* which I recorded in 1986. Earl was driving a Cadillac Eldorado. He was still working as a freelance musician and as an artist-in-residence for Osborne High School in Detroit. During the session, he told me that Motown pretty much dumped all the Funk Brothers in Detroit when the company moved to L.A. He said the only reason he still was doing okay financially was that his wife had saved and invested his money for him when things were still busy and going well.

Earl Van Dyke could jam and sight-read anything. He provided the full acoustic piano sound on all the Motown records. He created intricate chord voicings that provided the foundation that the guitars and bass used when they improvised. No matter how many guitars were on the session, Earl's acoustic piano could always be heard ringing out the chord patterns.

Sadly, Earl passed away in 1992. He still sounded great the last time I heard him, but he had arthritis in his hands and said they hurt a lot when he played. All of the Motown musicians kept in touch with Earl no matter where they lived. When I'd give him a call, he always had the latest information on the others and knew how they were doing.

The last time I saw Earl play was at the Montreux Jazz Festival in Detroit in 1991. He told me his hands hurt so much that he had to practice an hour each day in pain before he could get them limber enough to function. In spite of this, he still managed to perform and kept a busy, active schedule. Earl and I spoke briefly in the hallway at the festival, and I really felt bad because of the pain he was having. We shook hands for the last time as he walked toward the stage to do what he loved best. As I sat in the audience on that bright, summer day, soaking up the warm rays of the hot sun, I heard Earl play his music as usual—a master piano player until the very end.

James Jamerson was the number-one bass player at Motown. There wasn't a bass player in the world who could touch him. No one played like he did, and the only one I ever heard come close to his sound was his son, James Jr., when he brought out his father's Fender Precision bass to sit in on a gig I was playing in 1993. Not only did Jamerson hold down a groove with his funky bass lines in the rhythm section, but he played counterpoint melodies as he went from one chord to the next. Place any Motown record or CD on your system, turn up the bass, and listen to the way this guy was really playing. You'll be amazed at what you hear.

When Jamerson locked into a song, he put his heart and soul into it, and the outcome was simply incredible. Jamerson and I had a fierce musical kinship. We agreed on many things and were passionate about the different styles of music we played. We appreciated our individual uniqueness. In the sixties and seventies, Jamerson was probably the most respected R&B bass player in the world.

James Jamerson was the best friend I had at Motown. Not only was he the one, along with Hank Cosby, who offered me a job at the Producer's Workshop, but he also became my mentor.

I remember tossing down a few drinks in a bar with Jamerson from time to time, and we'd talk in my car after the bar closed. We'd debate music, share studio "war" stories, discuss jazz, and compare our styles of playing. Jamerson preached to me that you had to play what you felt and be true to your sound. He adhered to that principal all of his life, which is what made him such a musical giant.

One night Jamerson called me up and told me to meet him in this bar on Puritan Avenue in Detroit. It was a small shot and a beer joint, and when I got there the place was almost empty. Jamerson was sitting at the bar with a drink in his hand and a big grin on his face.

"Hey, man. What's so funny?" I asked as I sat down on the barstool.

Jamerson turned around and faced me with his drink still in one hand.

"I was minding my own business, walking down the street and

heading for the bar, when this guy came up and pointed a gun in my face. 'Gimme all your money,' he says."

"I couldn't believe he was serious," Jamerson went on. "Do you remember those Italian fountain pens we had that could fire .22 caliber bullets?"

I nodded. The pens looked like thick silver fountain pens but with one major difference. There was a catch on the side of the pen, and when you pulled it back it cocked the trigger mechanism and firing pin. The pen was now ready to fire a .22 caliber bullet from the front end, like one of James Bond's secret weapons. The pens would have probably blown up in our faces if we had ever tried to fire them. I think I lost mine when I left it in the pocket of a suit I sent out to the cleaners.

"Well," Jamerson went on, "I faked the asshole right out. I moved off to the side, put the pen behind his ear so he could feel the tip of the bullet. I told him, 'I got you covered pal—now, give me your gun!' So he gives me his gun. Once I got the damn gun away from him I said, 'Now give me YOUR money!' You should have seen the look on his face as he handed it over."

At the end of the story, Jamerson waved his hand in the air and grinned.

"The jerk didn't have that much money, but it's enough for us to buy a few rounds of drinks. Bartender, bring us over another round!"

Later I would continue to work with Jamerson at sessions in Los Angeles. I knew what it was like to switch from working with the same rhythm section in Detroit every day to playing with at least fifty different rhythm sections in L.A. I never really got used to it, and he didn't either.

Jamerson died there of pneumonia in 1983. James Jr. later stated, "My father would still be alive today if he had never moved to the West Coast. He should have never left Detroit!"

Like most large entertainment centers, the music scene in L.A. was fiercely competitive. Some people in the music business treated musicians like used cars; no matter what you did for them, they always had to try the latest model, which meant any new player in town with a few hit records under his or her belt.

Creative musicians are like fine-tuned athletes; it takes a lot of discipline and practice to become one of the best. I noticed in L.A. and New York that the arrangers took the time to write out elaborate parts. I never understood the reasoning behind that. A musician should be given the room and respect to be creative. When I used Jamerson to play bass on one of my albums at Crystal Studios in Hollywood, I wrote out a chord sheet and let him do his thing. I knew he would have been insulted if I'd written out a lot of complicated bass lines. I did have to write out one tune called "Mind Excursion" because it was a twelve-tone avant-garde piece with a lot of difficult bass parts, but Jamerson played the chart right on the money.

One of the last images I have of Jamerson is a flashback to a humid summer day at Motown's studio on Grand Boulevard in Detroit. We were jamming on a song, and I could see Jamerson playing his bass as I looked over my music stand. As usual, he was perched on his stool, a black beret tilted on the side of his head, while a lit cigarette dangled from his lips. I could still see him as he read the chart and moved back and forth to the groove of the music. He was punching out those outrageous bass lines, one foot stomping on the floor in time with the music and the other firmly anchored to the bottom rung of his stool. Welcome to the Motown Sound . . . courtesy of James Jamerson!

Bob Babbitt was another great player who worked with me at Motown. Bob was also the bass player behind the monster solo on my hit record "Scorpio." I played many sessions with Bob, including "Ball Of Confusion" by the Temptations. Bob has his own style and is still one hell of a bass player.

In the early seventies, a young guitarist named Melvin Ragin began playing on sessions before I went on the road with "Scorpio." Melvin saw me using a wah-wah pedal and began using one himself. Somehow, he got the nickname "Wah Wah" Watson, but I didn't mind. They say imitation is the sincerest form of flattery, and he always treated me respectfully.

When Jamerson first heard the nickname, he said "What kind of shit is that? You bring over a wah-wah pedal and use it on all those hits and this new guy is called Wah Wah?"

We welcomed "Wah Wah" to Hitsville, just like they welcomed me when I first came on the scene. The only Temptations hit I didn't play the wah-wah pedal on was "Papa Was A Rolling Stone," and Watson did a real bang-up job on that one.

Pistol Allen was one of the drummers who worked daily at Hitsville. Wiry and compact behind the drums, he wore black horn-rimmed glasses, which hinted at the serious side of his personality, a side also evident in his skill and technique when he played. Of course, Pistol could always crack a joke and make you laugh with a story or two. He was a precise drummer with fast hands, a lot of speed, and quick on the draw, which was how he got the nickname. Pistol was always a focused musician while playing and was a super nice guy as well.

Uriel Jones was the other drummer at Motown, and he played there every day. Uriel was stocky, muscular, and good with his hands. He was a great pocket drummer and always anchored the rhythm section down with his steady groove. He had one outstanding drum fill he used the most, which appeared on many Motown songs. The Cats always kidded Uriel and called it his "Pass the Biscuits" fill. I think they came up with the name because it was funky and had been served up on so many hits.

Both Pistol and Uriel still play the drums and work at local jazz clubs in the Metro Detroit area.

In the beginning at Motown, the main drummer was Benny Benjamin, but I worked with him only once. He was on the scene before my time.

"Bongo" Eddie Brown was the conga and bongo player at Motown. He was the studio clown and cutup. The killer weed that he sometimes smoked before the sessions or the girlie magazines he always had on his music stand could have been contributing factors to his jovial outlook on life. Bongo was a fantastic percussionist, and he kept us in stitches by cracking jokes in his imitation Bullwinkle voice. Bongo's comic relief helped us overcome the stress and daily pressures of recording different songs each day and trying to come up with hit records.

Bongo passed away at an early age after he also moved to L.A. I think living in L.A. might have added a lot of stress to his life. The last I heard he was working for Marvin Gaye on the road. I was one of the pallbearers at his funeral, which was held in Detroit. Looking down at Bongo in his casket brought back a lot of memories of us making great music together. Here I was in Bongo's old neighborhood again, but this time the circumstances were much sadder.

One of my memories was of a running joke we had in the studio. Sometimes we'd become so comfortable playing the same song over and over that our minds would begin to wander, and we'd begin making mistakes. When this happened, one of the Cats, like Eddie Willis, would call out, "Rig's sittin' in on the tune man!" "Rig" was short for rigor mortis. Bongo and everyone else would crack up, and that would clear the air so we could get back to work and return to playing the way we were supposed to.

Johnny Griffith was the other keyboard player at Motown. He had a wonderful sense of humor and often played electric organ on the sessions along with Earl's piano. Johnny had a degree in music and was—and still is—a talented player. He taught high school in Detroit but now lives in Las Vegas.

John Trudell was the trumpet player, and he led the horn section at Motown. John has a full head of gray hair, his kids are all grown, and he is still one of the busiest musicians in town. I used John on my horn dates, and he always played in tune and right on the money. He currently leads a band in Detroit and contracts with musicians for major shows around town.

Gordon Staples, the violin concertmaster at Motown, was a high-strung, artistic musician who played the sweetest violin I ever heard. He was the concertmaster for the Detroit Symphony Orchestra and the concertmaster for the string sections on my sessions as well. Gordon played a rare Stradivarius violin that resonated with a rich, mellow sound. When Gordon and his Strad were absent from a string section, you could really feel the difference.

Not only was Gordon a superb player, but he was an effective leader. If other members of the string section gave "The Rock & Roll Kid" a hassle during the session, they'd have to face Gordon the next day at the rehearsal for the symphony.

Gordon died of cancer shortly after he retired from the Detroit Symphony, and I never even knew he was sick. The last time I spoke with Gordon was in the symphony offices in the back of Ford Auditorium in Downtown Detroit after I came back from New York in need of a job. Gordon got me an interview for a position in symphony management. There was a fat chance that "The Rock & Roll Kid" would get a job with the symphony, but at least Gordon tried.

Jack Ashford was another percussionist who played at Motown every day. He was probably one of the few guys in the country who made a living playing tambourine. Jack began as a vibes player but later was in great demand in the studio as an expert playing rhythmic gospel tambourine, complementing the drum high hat and congas to produce the percussion for the Motown sound.

The last time I saw Jack at Motown he was playing tambourine in an overdub room and wearing a bright sport shirt hanging loosely outside of his dress slacks. Every time he lifted his tambourine up to play, I was surprised to see a huge .357 magnum revolver in a holster strapped to his belt. Most of us at Motown carried guns at one time or another because we worked at all hours of the night. We worked in recording studios and clubs and lived in dangerous times. At least I thought so back then, though now things seem to be even more violent.

We were all very visible and felt vulnerable because most of us drove brand new Fleetwood Broughams. We felt even more vulnerable at the studio, especially after one of the arrangers at Motown was severely beaten and robbed after a recording session. After that happened, we all carried guns in holsters or in our instrument cases.

Joe Messina was one of the original guitarists in the "Snake Pit." He was also a well-known jazz guitarist and had worked around the Detroit area for a long time. The first time I saw Joe play he was using his solid-body Fender Telecaster as a staff member of the *Soupy Sales* TV show. Before that he used to play on DJ Ed McKenzie's show. Most jazz guitarists in those days played hollow-body guitars like the Gibson 400 and L5, but Joe always loved his Telecaster. The bright sound of Joe's Telecaster came in handy when he played guitar backbeats for the sessions at Motown.

One of the main reasons why Motown hired Joe was that he could read just about any music placed in front of him. Most guitar funksters of that era could play real funky but left a lot to be desired in the sight-reading department. Guitars weren't used much in the public school music system back then. In the sixties and seventies, they were considered bastard instruments by the academic music community. One of my music theory instructors at Wayne State University smugly told me that he considered the greatest classical guitarist of this century, Andres Segovia, a little dry. I don't think he could have imagined that in the future a guitarist could drown out an entire symphony orchestra with a stack of the right amps. The guitar has always been the instrument of the working man because it is inexpensive and can be taken anywhere.

Joe Messina is now retired, but he plays jazz harmonica around town once in a while. In 1993, I was playing in a club and a complete stranger walked up to me and gave me a CD featuring Joe on harmonica and guitar. I listened to the CD when I got home, and Joe still sounded good.

Another guitarist who had been with Motown for a long time was Robert White. Robert was a husky guy who practiced karate in his spare time. As a result of this, he would come to Hitsville from time to time with one of his hands all bandaged up. I wouldn't take that kind of chance with my hands in those days, but Robert's hands always came through it all right. Robert always played a large, hollow body, Gibson L5 guitar and usually played with his thumb instead of with a guitar pick. He was a good guitar player and had a nice warm sound.

In 1994, I received a call from Wah Wah Watson, who was then living in L.A. Wah Wah had just returned from the hospital and told me that Robert had had a massive heart attack. He said that Robert was in a coma and it didn't look like he would survive. I found out later from Motown trumpet player John Trudell, that Robert had passed away. Robert was a good player and was always very friendly and outgoing when we worked together at Motown. I was sorry to hear of his passing.

Motown guitarist Eddie Willis, one the funkiest guitar players out there, was able to create his figures and fills because there were always other Motown guitarists to read the music and play the written guitar parts. Eddie played a Gibson 335 semihollow guitar most of the time.

Jack Brokenshaw was another percussionist. Jack played the vibes using four hard wooden mallets, two in each hand. He was an excellent musician, and previously well known as a member of the group the Australian Jazz Quintet. Jack began playing music in the land down under at the age of five and was an exceptional sight reader as well as a very animated jazz soloist. It was fascinating to watch him play the vibes onstage. During his solo, he would wave all four mallets in the air, flail at the vibes with maniacal frenzy, and play some of the fastest musical passages I ever heard. These days Jack owns a company that provides music for industrial films and videos. He is semiretired and lives in Florida. He still plays once a week down there with some retired jazz musicians from New York.

I often wondered why the Cats were pretty much ignored once Motown moved out and got settled in Los Angeles. When I moved out to L.A. on my own and Motown hired me to play sessions, I was the only one from Detroit, except occasionally for Wah Wah. Motown was using all new musicians.

Motown did not do as well in L.A. as it had in Detroit. In fact, by leaving the Cats behind, it lost the Motown Sound. In L.A., its records began to sound like all of the other records made on the West Coast. But the company did have some success. It was in California that Motown discovered Lionel Richie and broke the Jackson Five, who I first met at the studio in Detroit when we were cutting tracks for them. But Michael and Janet Jackson did not become superstars until they went with other labels, and after Michael left the Jackson Five faded from the public eye.

In L.A., Berry was just another small independent record label executive lacking the money and resources to compete with big guns such as MCA, Capitol, and Warner Brothers. These labels forced the smaller independents out of business by controlling their distribution or buying them outright.

The complete collapse of the independents during the seventies came after RCA bought the distribution rights to A&M and MCA bought the rights to distribute Motown records. At that time, most of the large independent distributors in the country, including AMI Distributors in Detroit, went belly up. After that, record distribution throughout the world was controlled by six international conglomerates, which prohibited the development of many new and innovative musical ideas and kept new artists to a minimum. This new record cartel was made up of WEA (Warner Brothers, Atlantic, and Elektra), MCA, RCA, Capitol/EMI, PolyGram, and Columbia.

After the seventies and the Motown Sound became just a sweet memory, the best thing I could say about Berry Gordy was that he was a musical visionary and a shrewd businessman. He was the only record label owner who created a major global entertainment business in Detroit, and with very limited resources. I disagreed with some of his business tactics and loyalties, but they proved to be effective for Motown. I was proud to have played a part in the Motown Sound but was saddened by the way the company treated the musicians after it had moved to California.

What exactly constituted the Motown Sound? One of the things the Motown Sound had was consistency—when you heard it on the radio, you knew right away that it was Motown. The Motown Sound was the total sum of many specific components, the first of which was the original drummer, Benny Benjamin, nicknamed Papa Cita. When I came to work at Motown, Benny was already too sick to work because his body was weak and ravaged by illness.

Benny usually played with an unpretentious drum set that featured a small bass drum, high hat, ride cymbal, and snare. In 1966, I had the opportunity to play with Benny during an all-night session at Golden World, which featured him and Jamerson, both playing in defiance of Motown.

During the session, Benny appeared to be nodding out against the wall behind his drum set, even as he played. He looked worn out, but his playing was right on. He never missed a beat. Benny was a very funny guy, and he had a million hilarious excuses to explain why he was always late. In the studios in Detroit, the African American guys would joke and tell anyone who was late for a recording session that they must be on CPT, which stood for colored people time. Eventually that became the standard excuse for anyone who came in late.

The last time I saw Benny Benjamin was at his funeral. They laid him out at Cole's Funeral Home next to the Hitsville studios. He looked pretty bad because he had lost a lot of weight. During a break from a recording session, we stood in front of his casket and paid our respects. I didn't know him that well, but the pained look I saw on the faces of the band members demonstrated how difficult it must have been for them.

After Benny Benjamin stopped playing, Motown began using two drummers on every session. Pistol Allen played double-time, syncopated, high-hat rhythms, while Uriel Jones played snare drum and foot pedal, the same drum combination that I used for "Scorpio." On the Motown records, Pistol and Uriel blended and played so well together that I don't think anyone outside of Motown or Detroit knew that there were two drummers. When Motown combined this polyrhythmic, two-drummer approach with Jack Ashford's rhythmic gospel tambourine and Bongo Eddie's congas, it produced an electrifying sound made up of counterpoint rhythms complementing each other.

Another interesting element in the Motown Sound was the guitar backbeat. I don't know who came up with it, but most of the Motown records had a sharp-sounding guitar part played high up on the neck along with the beat of the snare drum. I know Joe Messina played a lot of backbeats in the early sixties, but Eddie Willis and I played them too. In order to play the backbeat, you needed a solid-body guitar for that sharp clean sound, and Joe, Eddie, and I all had them. Robert White never played the backbeat part because he had a hollow-body Gibson, which produced a real mellow sound and didn't cut through like a solid body.

Another critical element in the Motown Sound was the funky, hollow sound of the bass played by James Jamerson. James always played his electric bass with the strings real high off the fingerboard like an upright bass, which he also used to play. He never changed his strings unless one broke. When James played the funk, you could feel it on each record. He also played melodically throughout the chord changes and added syncopated rhythms to his bass lines as well. Later on at Motown the arrangers provided bass parts for him to read, but when I used him in L.A. on my *Instant Coffey* album, I gave him a lot of freedom to play whatever he wanted to and he came up with some incredible bass parts.

Another element in the Motown Sound were the songs themselves. Some of the hit songs at Motown just dripped with commercial, melodic hooks. The songs written by major talents such as Smokey Robinson, Holland-Dozier-Holland, Ashford & Simpson,

Norman Whitfield, and Barrett Strong had very innovative and melodic chord changes for the times. The jazz-style chords and voicings in the music reflected the rich heritage of the writers, the studio musicians, and the city of Detroit. Today you can still hear live bands in Detroit clubs playing everything, including jazz, R&B, blues, rock, country, and Top 40.

One final element in the Motown Sound was the lush orchestra with horns and strings that appeared on so many Motown records. This musical approach, known as "sweetening," added a pop crossover appeal, which made the funky R&B rhythm section on some records sound almost like mainstream pop. The Motown Sound was an urban slick sound for the times, and in terms of record sales it competed successfully with the polished sounds of L.A., New York, and Chicago and even with the Philadelphia-International Sound of producers Gamble and Huff.

While listening to the music playbacks in the control room, I also noticed that the Motown engineers added the echo and equalization right on the tape when they were cutting rhythm tracks. At least that was how it appeared because it sounded exactly like every Motown record I ever heard on the radio. I think Berry kept defining and redefining the Motown Sound until he became successful and then stuck with it. Berry probably picked up the idea of standardization from working on the assembly line at the Ford Motor Company in his early years. Even today it's kind of difficult to find anyone in Detroit who hasn't worked on an automotive assembly line at one time or another.

Some people said we punched out records day after day with the same corporate sound. Motown used the same musicians and equalization on each record and turned out so many products that it may have seemed that way to outsiders. But I've worked on a factory assembly line at General Motors, and I can guarantee you that Motown was different. Making records at Motown was a very creative process in which the whole was greater than the sum of the individual parts.

The Motown Sound evolved the way it did because it was a regional sound that reflected the lives and experiences of the musicians who played it. The music had a funky feel, but because of the complex chord changes in the songs the music went beyond being just another regional blues sound. Most of the vocalists at Motown had a slick, urban sound to their voices, which was different from the blues singers and southern funk singers who came out of Stax in Memphis and farther south. This vocal sound provided Motown with enormous pop crossover appeal, especially with groups like Diana Ross and the Supremes.

Each week there was a quality control meeting consisting of a panel made up of Motown hit producers and writers. Before a record could be released, the panel voted on it. The panel had to give its approval or the record never came out. Sometimes the panel would recommend that the producer make specific changes. The producer then made the changes and brought the record back for review at another meeting. I sometimes wondered how much internal Motown politics had to do with the voting.

In the seventies, one of the music trade magazines listed the value of Motown Records at $70 million and the value of its Jobete publishing company at another $70 million. If Motown hadn't frozen out the competition in Detroit, all the musicians would have been making double scale and playing ten sessions per week like the "A Team" musicians are doing now in Nashville. At $500 per session, or $5,000 per week at union scale, that adds up to $260,000 per year. When Motown left Detroit, the end result was Berry Gordy and Motown $140 million, musicians nil.

Given all of Motown's success, I only wish that the musicians could have shared more of the profits from both the sale of the records and the amount of radio and TV airplay the company received over the years. Earl Van Dyke once told me that there was something in the works that would give musicians residuals every time Motown records were played, but I knew that would never happen. If any musician got paid every time his music was played, anywhere in the world, we'd all be rich men today.

If you were a staff musician working every day for Motown, you signed exclusively with them and they paid you a weekly salary based on the number of sessions they expected you to do. If you made more money by doing more sessions, they paid you the difference at the end of the year.

Each musician had an escrow fund, which paid his salary and

kept track of his sessions. The musicians also had health insurance, but they had to relinquish the right to work for anyone else, which kept all of the major record labels from opening studios or offices in Detroit. When Motown left everyone high and dry by moving to California, we really came to understand the consequences of having no other record companies in town.

Every musician who entered into that type of agreement with Motown should have been given a pension fund of $25,000 or $30,000 per year plus medical benefits. They were company men and worked exclusively for Motown. There is a small pension fund, administered by the Musician's Union, intended for freelance musicians but not for company musicians. Motown was so secretive about its agreements with the musicians that I don't think the union even knew all the details. I'm glad I didn't get caught up in that kind of deal. In those days, many music companies treated their personnel that way but with one major difference: they didn't prevent them from making extra money on the side.

The entire time I worked for Motown as a freelancer in Detroit, I received one bonus, a pair of binoculars for Christmas, which I still have. But, unlike others, I was able to work the other labels too. I was also getting a production salary from Sussex Records and artist and writer royalties.

One day back in the early seventies, Harry Balk, who used to produce Del Shannon, called me into a meeting at Motown.

"We know you've been doing a lot of sessions for Holland, Dozier, and Holland since they left Motown," Harry said as he puffed on his cigar.

At the time, HDH were beginning to score hits with acts such as Freda Payne, Chairmen Of The Board, and the Honey Cone. I played on all of those records. Motown was a little uptight because HDH had financial backing and were recording a lot of hits at their own studio in the old Tower Theater at Grand River and Meyers in Detroit. In fact, I was at HDH recording every night after the Motown Producer's Workshop. At the time, I was doing fifteen to eighteen recording sessions a week. I was also playing at night with a jazz group and doing production work. I was earning about $70,000 per year, which was big money in 1970 dollars.

"We've been giving you a lot of work" Harry continued, "if you count the recording sessions and Producer's Workshop. If you want to keep working for us, stop making records for Holland-Dozier-Holland!"

"I don't have an exclusive agreement with Motown," I said, "and I'm not on your escrow system, so the answer's real simple. As a free agent, I can work for anyone I want to, including HDH. If Motown doesn't like it, don't call me! No problem, case closed."

I was beginning to get a little hot under the collar by then, so I turned and walked out of his office and slammed the door behind me.

I continued to work for HDH, which didn't seem to make a big difference at Motown. Within a week or two, they were calling me again to play on all the sessions.

One day I was playing guitar on a recording session for HDH at Tera Shirma. This was before HDH their own studio. As I was getting ready to go into the studio, I saw a tough, swarthy-looking guy and his henchmen using a video camera to film everyone as they entered the studio. Someone told me the swarthy guy was the head of Motown security.

By this time, I'd had about enough of Motown's strong-arm tactics, so I mugged in front of the camera and did my interpretation of a vaudeville soft-shoe routine and laughed in their faces. I wish I could have seen their expressions when they watched that segment of the film or tried to use it in court as evidence.

In the end, the Motown musicians had nothing but disappointment and disillusionment to show for being loyal company men—no pension, no security, no nothing. When the Motown era was finally over and one of the greatest recording bands of all time was laid to rest, you could still hear the faint echoes of guitar backbeats, funky bass lines, and drums beating in the distance, calling out for recognition, justice, and fair play. Although many other fine musicians played at Motown before I got there, I can only speak about the ones who worked with me.

Scorpio

My first attempt to enter show business was at the age of fourteen, when I auditioned for the Ed McKenzie TV show on Channel 7 in Downtown Detroit. I was dressed in a light gray suit with a one-button roll, pegged pants, a yellow knit tie, and blue suede shoes. I had my hair slicked down with a Tony Curtis curl in the front and a duck's ass in the back. Man, I sure thought I was hot stuff. Into the TV studio I carried my amp and my black, solid-body electric guitar with tiny silver speckles that flashed in the sunlight like finely cut diamonds. I intended to play guitar and sing "Blue Suede Shoes" to get a spot in the talent contest on the show.

When I got to the station, WXYZ, I was jammed together with a cattle call of bright young hopefuls. We were all reaching up to grasp the brass ring of stardom and the fantastic riches and public adulation that come with it. When my turn came to perform, unluckily for me, I was almost completely overcome with stage fright. I was so scared and nervous that I could hardly function. I'm sure my fear and apprehension were quite evident to the producers of the show because I bombed out. They rejected me right then and there, like a jilted lover on a first date. I had worked so hard singing to records and practicing guitar riffs that I felt suddenly betrayed and devastated. I lost all confidence in myself and thought that maybe I wasn't show business material after all.

Weeks later, after I got over the disappointment of blowing the audition, I went to a department store and bought a tape recorder, which was the newest invention to hit the audio market. This new gadget cost me about thirty dollars, and was real small and compact. It sounded tinny, like the first transistor radios made in Japan, but I was totally captivated with it. I spent hours recording sounds off the radio, and then used my newfound toy to learn the vocals and guitar parts. One day I recorded my voice on tape, played it back, and really listened to the sound. My voice was nasally and uninteresting, and I didn't think I would ever make it as a singer.

At that moment, I made the decision that changed my life forever: if I couldn't be a great singer, I'd devote all my energies to becoming the best guitar player I could, and that's what I did. With years of practice, the strategy finally paid off. After my first recording contract as part of a duo, my second contract under the name Clark Summit, and my contract with the Royaltones, in 1969 I was offered a fourth recording contract, which proved to be the catalyst for my entire career. This contract was under my own name and was with Venture Records, a label owned by MGM.

Recording contracts are usually complicated documents, and they can contain as many as fifty pages or more. The terms of the contract are very specific to the recording industry, so you need to hire an attorney familiar with industry jargon and its standard business practices to explain what each term really means. After my contract was signed, I went into the studio to record my first album with Mike Theodore at the control board, Lyman Woodard on organ, Melvin Davis on drums, and Bob Babbitt on bass. I wanted to record an entire album, because with an album you at least have your choice of one of ten songs for a single. When you record three songs for a single session, you only have the choice of one song out of three.

We decided to record an album based on things, such as "Do Your Thang," "It's Your Thing," "Iceberg's Thang," and songs from the musical *Hair*, such as "Let The Sunshine," and "Aquarius." We called the album *Hair And Thangs*, and Venture Records released it along with "It's Your Thing" as a single.

Unfortunately, Venture Records was drowning in red ink, and although MGM brought in record executive Clarence Avant to try to save it he came onboard too late. MGM shut the label down.

Without a major national promotional effort, *Hair And Thangs* died a quiet and peaceful death throughout the country, but the single; "It's Your Thing," was a number-one record in Detroit. At the time, I was out promoting the record and performing at record hops at the Twenty Grand Ballroom for DJs such as WJLB's "Frantic" Ernie Durham, Jay Butler, and WCHB's Ken Bell.

In 1992, I played at a reunion for Lyman Woodard at Sully's bar on Greenfield in Dearborn and "Frantic" Ernie was there. I had just finished playing a set with Lyman, and I was walking toward the dressing room, when I saw the "Frantic One" sitting at the bar. Even though I hadn't seen him in years, Ernie still looked stylish and debonair in his tie and sharp blue sports jacket with brown slacks. I sat down on a barstool next to him, and we reminisced about old times for about half an hour. We discussed various people we knew and what they were doing now. When I read in the paper a few weeks later that Ernie had passed away, I couldn't believe it. He was a radio legend, a real nice guy, and he will be missed. I was glad I got to talk to him about the old days one last time.

I really worked hard to promote "It's Your Thing." I did radio interviews, promoted the song at the club, and when it became number one on WJLB I began to do concerts at union halls, which led to doing concerts at Cobo Hall and Ford Auditorium.

The first time I appeared at Cobo Hall, the excitement and stress was unbelievable. The concert was promoted by Frank Brown and featured many popular R&B acts in the area. Frank was an experienced show promoter who blasted out ads on television and in the newspapers. After one of Frank's high-profile media blitzes, you couldn't help but become a household name.

Frank knew what the people in his market wanted to hear, and he booked the acts on his shows accordingly. He then rented the facility and packed them in like sardines. I think the capacity of Cobo Hall at the time was about fifteen thousand people.

Frank was no dummy when it came to collecting the ticket receipts. He had two bodyguards carrying pump shotguns, who followed him around the ticket offices where the money was kept. To my knowledge, Frank was never robbed.

That night I was the opening act for the Temptations, who at the time were one of Motown's hottest groups. It was very hard to hear the music onstage because of the immense size of the stage and audi-torium. As I looked out into the crowd, I could see faceless rows of people, which seemed to rise up out of the floor and go on forever until they disappeared in the glare of the lights somewhere in the dark ceiling of the auditorium.

In the beginning, I was terrified onstage in front of a crowd of fif-teen thousand people in the blinding glare of the stage lights. I was using a huge stack of Marshall and Fender guitar amplifiers, which were popular in the sixties. They could really kick out the decibels, but at this concert the public address system was not really equipped to handle such volume, which made it hard to hear the drums onstage and some of the other instruments, such as the bass. Well, as they say in show business, "The show must go on," and we played and received thunderous applause from a packed house.

I know that if Venture Records had not gone belly up "It's Your Thing" would have been a huge national hit, maybe not as big as "Scorpio" but at least in the Top 10 on *Billboard's* Top 100 R&B chart.

After the demise of Venture Records, which not only fumbled the ball on my album but lost the first album Mike and I produced on Rare Earth, Clarence Avant telephoned to say that he was starting a new label called Sussex Records in L.A., with Buddha Records as the distributor. He offered to sign Rare Earth and me to the label and also offered Mike and me staff producer positions. This was the big break we had been waiting for, so we agreed and began planning a new album.

The Sussex distributor, Buddha Records, began as a bubble gum label in New York and was conceived by Art Kass and music maven Neil Bogart. Neil was like P. T. Barnum: a promoter first and a record man second. He was responsible for discovering acts like Kiss and disco diva Donna Summer. Neil was always fascinated with the real "Bogey," Humphrey Bogart. Later, when he moved out to L.A., he began another record label and named it Casablanca. He used to run full-page ads in *Billboard* promoting the label, which showed him dressed in a hat and trench coat like his favorite star.

The *Scorpio* album began with me in the basement, writing songs and recording them on a Sony Sound-on-Sound stereo tape recorder. In that way, I was able to record multiple tracks and ping pong them back and forth, overlaying different parts into a stereo two-track mix.

I came up with the idea of using a guitars in a different way on this album. I orchestrated them like horns and strings and layered them in sections. I decided to call the album Evolution in reference to this innovative use of guitars. I also decided to call my backup group, the Detroit Guitar Band, which really didn't exist yet because studio musicians played all of the parts on the album.

On the song "Scorpio," I used a guitar horn section composed of nine guitars playing the melody in three different octaves. Ray Monette from Rare Earth, Joe Podorsek, and I played the horn parts I had written as well as the string-type parts on guitars. I overdubbed each section three different times, and each time we changed octaves and parts. I used fourths to achieve that unique spatial sound in the melody. I even played a bass guitar through a fuzz tone and wah-wah pedal to imitate a trombone and baritone saxophone.

In the rhythm section, I used my session mates, the Motown "A Team, the Funk Brothers": Earl Van Dyke on piano, Uriel Jones and Pistol on drums, "Bongo" Eddie on congas, and Jack Ashford on tambourine. It was a star-studded, righteous rhythm section made up of musicians with successful track records a mile long. Apparently the executives at Motown didn't hear about the session until afterward. They were so busy watching Jamerson and the guitar players that when I played guitar and used Bob Babbitt on bass they were caught completely off guard.

I wrote out the basic music arrangements, which I directed while facing the band and playing guitar at the same time. In the middle of "Scorpio," I gave the band a percussion breakdown that climaxed with a violent bass solo by Bob Babbitt. The breakdown was also sprinkled throughout with raucous and soulful comments by Bongo Eddie and Jack Ashford, who added vocal ad-libs that accidentally filtered onto the sound tracks through their instrument microphones. On the record, you can hear Bongo yelling, "Grab it Babbitt!"

Mike Theodore was the first one to notice the value in it. "Hey that's great!" Mike said, a big grin on his face. "I love it. Leave it in."

On the session, I gave these boys some room and just let the

horses run, and you can hear the results on the record. All the musicians on the session were given a basic musical arrangement as a
guide, but when I opened the song up for breakdowns and solos they
went wild. I knew how they felt. When Norman Whitfield gave me
some room in a solo on a Temptations' record, I just closed my eyes,
leaned back and let 'er rip.

Evolution was released to everyone's high expectations but died
a slow painful death and went under with barely a ripple. I was totally
devastated and couldn't figure out what in the hell had gone wrong.
We had major distribution, and everyone was promoting the record,
and yet it still turned out to be a dud! My failure was beginning to
turn into a bad habit.

It took me a while to get over my disappointment, but the next
year rolled around and Clarence at Sussex agreed to pop for another
album. Mike Theodore and I decided to retire the Detroit Guitar
Band concept, hire a real orchestra, and record a few cover songs as
well. We titled the album *Going For Myself* and planned to record
some of my originals and cover songs such as "Bridge Over Troubled
Water" by Paul Simon and "It's Too Late" by Carole King.

We used horns, strings, and male and female background singers
on this album and a new, non-Motown rhythm section. Two of the
background singers were Telma Hopkins and Joyce Vincent, who
became Tony Orlando's backup group Dawn.

The rhythm section I used for the *Going For Myself* album was
the road band I had put together to perform promotional tours.
There was Bob Babbitt and Tony Newton on bass, Eric Morgenson
on keyboards, Andrew Smith on drums, James Barnes on congas, and
me on guitar. I also used Jack Ashford on percussion to add a little
Motown flavor to the sound in the studio.

We went into the studio and recorded a new album with the
background singers and orchestra, but before the scheduled release
date something very unusual happened. I got a call from Ron
Mosley, Sussex's national promotion man in New York.

"Hey, Dennis," Ron said, hardly containing his excitement. "I
went into a dance club in midtown Manhattan three weeks ago and
the people were dancing and going nuts over 'Scorpio'!"

"Man, I thought that album had stiffed," I said, wondering what was going on.

"I reserviced the clubs and stores here in New York with the *Evolution* album," Ron continued, "and the record is beginning to get requests like crazy! I'm going to get Clarence to release Scorpio as a single."

Now he had me excited. Ron was an experienced promotion man, and when he got excited about something it was for real.

"Well, lets get it out then," I agreed.

Based on Ron's recommendation, Sussex released "Scorpio" as a single and the rest was musical history.

I remember sitting in a bar in Detroit on Eight Mile Road one night with Mike Theodore. Since "Scorpio" was currently number fifteen on WJLB, I went out to my car to listen to their new countdown and see what position the record would have this week. I must have sat in my car for at least half an hour. Each time a record was played and its new position was announced and I didn't hear "Scorpio," I got more nervous and apprehensive. The closer to number one the DJ got with the conspicuous absence of "Scorpio," the more depressed I felt. Because the *Evolution* album had stiffed, I began to get real bad vibes about the WJLB countdown. I began thinking to myself, what if the damn record fell off the countdown completely? What would happen then?

As I sat there getting more depressed and resigning myself to the fact that this was probably the end of the road for "Scorpio," like some of my previous failures, I suddenly heard the big drum roll for record number one. I was thinking to myself that at least Scorpio had reached number fifteen, when my ears picked up a faint familiar sound slowly building in the background.

At the end of the drum roll, the voice of the disc jockey cut in.

"And now," he announced, "up from number fifteen last week, the new number one record in the Motor City by Dennis Coffey, 'Scorpio'!"

When I heard that, I almost fell out of the car. Scorpio had gone from number fifteen to number one in one week! Most records move up a few positions a week or maybe one or two positions when they get in the top five, but "Scorpio" had blown the competition away to jump fourteen places and take the number-one slot!

When the record was over, I got out of the car and ran into the bar to tell Mike. He was still sitting on his stool having a drink and talking to the barmaid.

"Man, can you believe it?" I yelled. "It's jumped all the way from fifteen to number one in one week on 'JLB."

"It looks like 'Scorpio' is gonna be a major hit," I kept going. "I can't remember a record moving that fast up the charts. Mosley was right, we have a hit on our hands!"

Mike and I stayed in the bar until closing time, celebrating one of the most memorable nights in my career.

The next week I received a call from Sussex Records.

"We have to delay the release date on *Going For Myself* because "Scorpio" is going up the national charts like a speeding bullet and selling records like crazy. We want you to go back in the studio and resurrect the Detroit Guitar Band and give us three new cuts."

I agreed and wrote and recorded three new songs. One of those songs was called "Taurus," which charted in the Top 10 in *Cashbox* and the Top 20 in *Billboard* when we later released it as a follow-up single to "Scorpio." When *Going For Myself* was finally released, there were three songs on it featuring the Detroit Guitar Band: "Taurus," "Can You Feel It?" and "Ride Sally Ride." "Ride Sally Ride" also hit the Top 50 in *Billboard.*

I was sitting with my dad in the Sussex office in New York when the final order came in that pushed "Scorpio" to over a million in sales. One of the guys in the office took the order over the telephone from a record distributor. We both went nuts. It was my very first gold record! Later, when Sussex issued gold record awards as mementos to celebrate our success, I got one for my dad and my mom, and they both hung them on their living room walls with pride. Not bad for a kid who grew up running the streets of Detroit and who never thought he'd get paid anything for playing music—let alone win the most coveted symbol of success in the music business.

Taking It on the Road

As the record continued to climb the charts, I got a call from a promoter in New York by the name of Sparky. Sparky offered me a gig to play one night in the ballroom at a hotel in Brooklyn. Ron Mosley thought it would be good promotion for the record.

I rehearsed the band and rented a truck that my dad agreed to drive. Then we loaded up our equipment and headed for Brooklyn.

We had arrived in New York and my dad was driving the truck through Central Park when a yellow cab unexpectedly came speeding out of the rain. He didn't have enough time to stop, and our truck scraped the entire side of the cab with the front bumper. Except for a slightly bent bumper, we had no other visible damage. The damage to the cab was another story. After we stopped, the driver jumped out and looked at the car and shook his head.

"No problem," he said.

Then he got back in his cab, started the engine, and careered off into the rainy night. I looked at the truck.

"Welcome to New York," I said to my dad.

That night we pulled up to a large gray hotel situated on a busy intersection teeming with people. We walked in and asked the desk clerk where we could park the truck. He looked up at us and grinned sheepishly.

"I'd tell you to see our parking lot attendant," he said, "but someone blew his face away with a shotgun last night, so you'd better park outside next to the building. Back your truck up, take out your distributor cap, chain the steering wheel and you should be all right," he concluded, and then went back to reading his newspaper. Nervously, we followed his advice and then went to our rooms to try to get some shuteye.

Miraculously, when we checked on the truck in the morning it was still intact. That night the grand ballroom was packed, and we were the headline act. Toward the end of the set, we went into "Scorpio," and were really surprised at what happened next. We began playing the song, and I looked out at the audience and saw this huge conga line forming and moving toward the stage. It slithered back and forth like a gigantic snake.

When the line reached the stage, I saw the faces of happy people in seventh heaven cavorting and dancing their butts off. I finally got the opportunity to see firsthand the effect "Scorpio" had on a crowd of people on a dance floor. No wonder it had created such a stir in the dance clubs in New York. That's what always made the music business so special; you could always expect the unexpected.

Bob Babbitt, the bassist in the band, was large and boisterous, and his frequent outbursts of energy and threats of violence were well known in the record industry. In New York City, he once threatened to throw a record promotion man out of a second-story window. He had actually grabbed the man and was carrying him toward the window before he thought better of it. Bob was a really a good guy at heart, but every so often he blew his stack.

Once, when the band boarded a plane to take us to a concert, Bob took it upon himself to address the passengers before the plane took off. At the time, Babbitt was dressed in a funky ripped T-shirt and jeans. He was also wearing an old black beret covered with white spots that looked suspiciously like bird droppings—which they probably were. As we were boarding the plane, Bob stopped at the front of the aisle and smiled. He addressed the passengers in his best imitation pilot voice.

"Good afternoon, ladies and gentlemen," Bob said, with a deep rumble in his throat. "My name is Bob, and I'll be your pilot today. We will be cruising at approximately twenty thousand feet, and our scheduled arrival time is 5:30 P.M. Have a safe flight."

An old lady in an aisle seat sniffled into a white handkerchief.

"My god," she mumbled. "He can't really be the pilot. We're all gonna die!"

Bob smiled at her nonchalantly, winked, and slowly moved his impressive bulk down the aisle toward his seat, while the rest of the passengers stared blankly toward the front of the plane in nervous silence.

Another time we had just finished an outdoor concert on the Commons in downtown Boston and had gone back to our hotel. We had added an excellent singer, Sam Calle, to our band, and I was really happy with the show that night. At about three in the morning, we received a telephone call. Our drummer, Andrew Smith, answered the phone and talked for a while. Then he hung up and went back to sleep.

The next morning we were eating breakfast when I noticed Bob was missing.

"Hey, guys," I looked up and asked between bites, "where the hell is Babbitt? He usually doesn't stay out all night without telling us."

Andrew looked at me kind of sheepishly.

"Damn," he said. "I think I spoke to him on the phone last night. He called and said he was in jail for assault or something and asked if we could bail him out. I thought I was dreaming," Andrew said, as he chewed. "I must have fallen right back to sleep. I sure know we didn't go to jail last night and bail him out."

We all stared at each other for a minute as visions appeared of this huge, irate bass player in a ripped T-shirt with bird shit on his hat smacking the crap out of everyone within reach. We dropped our food and scrambled for the door.

"Let's get out of here," I yelled. "I sure don't want to be here when he does get out." We made a mad rush for the door and stayed away from the room all day to give Babbitt a chance to cool down. When we got back that afternoon, he was in the room waiting for us. He was pretty calm as he related what had happened to him on the previous night.

It seems Bob had been walking down the street, minding his own business, when he happened to pass a bar where a few customers were standing outside, catching an ocean breeze on a hot summer night. One of the guys said something insulting to Bob as he passed. Apparently, Bob took offense. The police were called to quell the disturbance, and Bob took offense at them too. There were four policemen in two separate squad cars, and it seems they in turn took offense at Bob and "Rodney Kinged" him about the face and body before shoving him into the squad car and taking him off to jail. It must have been quite a major donnybrook with Babbitt, two barflies, and four policemen swinging billy clubs. I wonder what the people on the street thought!

Once the police had Babbitt in the slammer, he was allowed one phone call, which was answered by Andrew, who promptly hung up and went back to sleep.

James Barnes, our conga player, seemed to have relatives in every major city in which we appeared. One day we'd be driving through the Bronx in New York, and he'd tell us to pull over.

"Hey, there's my cousin," James would yell. "Let me out. I need to talk to him." I'd stop the car and open the door and James would jump out and disappear onto a street full of pedestrians.

It didn't seem to matter what city we were in, James would still ask us to stop. "Hey, I got relatives that live by this corner. Let me out."

He would jump out of the car and show up later back at the hotel. Sometimes he'd have a relative in tow when he returned, and he would introduce him or her to us as cousin so and so.

One night we were staying in adjoining rooms in a hotel on Broadway in New York. In the middle of the night, I was rudely awakened by loud, horrible screams of terror coming from the room next door. I jumped out of bed and ran over and opened the door to see what the hell was going on. As I looked in, I was horrified to see a body on the floor covered with blood, contorted grotesquely.

For one heart-stopping moment, I was frozen in time. The rest of the band joined me. We all had the same reaction. We thought it was James lying there.

I finally got a grip on myself and walked over to the body. Just then, James jumped out of the closet, laughing like hell. Only then did I noticed that the body was a cleverly made dummy dressed in James' shirt and pants, with a fake head covered with ketchup. At the time, we were so angry that we almost turned James into a real dead body.

"What in the hell is wrong with you?" I yelled. "Have you lost your mind? You not only scared the shit out of us," I screamed even louder, "but you woke me up out of a sound sleep. I really don't appreciate your sense of humor."

James looked at me nonchalantly and shrugged his shoulders.

"What's a matter," he mumbled, "can't you guys take a joke?"

I vowed to myself right then and there that I would never have a room next to anyone in the band again. It turned out to be a smart move on my part because it saved my ass during the next episode of "On the Road with the Detroit Guitar Band."

We had just performed at a club in Washington, D.C. The crowd there was awesome, and the concert went off without a hitch. On the way back, I noticed what appeared to be about ten squad cars surrounding our hotel.

"Man," I said, "someone must have gotten whacked in the hotel to bring out that many of Washington's finest."

We got out of our cab and proceeded to walk through the lobby and go up to our rooms. I didn't notice it at the time, but the lobby was awfully quiet. I left the rest of the guys and walked down the hall to my room to relax and watch a little TV. I had just sat down and turned on the TV when I got a frantic telephone call from Andrew.

"Man," he whispered, "there's big trouble over here in front of the roadies' room. You'd better get down here fast!"

I couldn't imagine what was going on, but the urgency I heard Andrew's voice got me moving fast.

As I walked around the corner of the hallway that led to the room where my roadies were staying, I couldn't believe my eyes. The entire hallway seemed to be filled with policemen. There were both patrolmen and plainclothes detectives standing and milling around. The center of attention seemed to be my two roadies, Mark and Steve, who were looking downcast and dejected and wearing handcuffs. I walked over to a sullen-faced, beefy detective to find out what was going on, but Andrew had already begun to argue with him. The detective told both of us to shut up. At that point, we wisely heeded his advice and stopped talking. He further informed us that the guys in handcuffs were headed off to jail on a drug charge and if we wanted to join them he'd be more than happy to oblige.

When I finally unraveled the entire story, it seemed that my two roadies had left some minor evidence of pot and pills out in plain view in their rooms. When they were away from their rooms, helping us during our concert, the hotel maid saw the stuff and alerted the hotel manager, who must have called the police.

I don't believe in using drugs, so I wasn't very sympathetic to their excuses. When my roadies got out on bail, I pretty much ignored the whole thing. I was beginning to tire of life on the road, and I was thinking of dissolving the band and going back to Detroit. I still had kids at home to raise and a production company to run with Mike Theodore. The road didn't seem like such a viable option to me anymore, especially since the expenses of traveling on weekends all over the country to perform at concerts was eating us alive. Although I was playing concerts at the Philharmonic in New York and McCormack Place in Chicago, performing in huge, echoing concert halls before large audiences was more suited to a rock band than me. I still favored the intimacy of a small concert hall or jazz club.

My first attempt to get on a TV show at the age of fourteen had bombed out. Fortunately, I got a second chance. When I was with the Royaltones, we had a huge local following in Detroit, and we appeared on the shows *Swingin' Time* and *Club 1270* to promote our new records. In those days, most television stations didn't have the equipment to broadcast a live band, so most featured artists pantomiming to their records.

My next venture into the world of television came in 1967, when I had a staff position on the *Tom Shannon Show* on Channel 9 in Windsor, Ontario, across the bridge from Detroit. Channel 9 was located in a long brick building along with its sister station, CKLW radio. You could look out of the window, past the parking lot, and see the Detroit River flowing toward Lake Erie, with waves twinkling in the sun against the Detroit skyline.

One of the hardest things to get used to on television was the amount of lighting needed to remove the shadows from the soundstage. There were so many bright lights generating so much heat that it became almost unbearable. We could hardly wait for the commercial breaks so we could get out of the hot lights and cool off.

Mike Theodore and I were hired to contract musicians. We also wrote arrangements for the band, with Mike conducting and me on guitar. The band was made up of Canadian and American musicians, and we were on TV five days a week. We used Pistol Allen on drums, Bob Babbitt on bass, and Johnny Griffith on piano. We hired three horn players from Windsor to provide the horn section. On the show, we provided music for the guest artists and created short musical chasers to play between scenes when they went to commercials and station IDs.

The show was on in the sixties, when hippies and the Haight Asbury look were in. I went down to Plum Street, downtown near Tiger Stadium, which was Detroit's coffeehouse and hippie district, and bought the appropriate bell bottoms and hippie outfits to make me look fashionable.

The show lasted only eight weeks, but we enjoyed every minute of it. We got to meet some interesting people, such as Joe Cocker and Three Dog Night. But it wasn't until "Scorpio" took off and began climbing the national charts that I was invited to appear on national, rather than just local, TV.

First was *Soul Train*, with host Don Cornelius. We were scheduled to perform live, so we flew to L.A. on a 747 to do the show. Back then, 747s were all the rage. They were huge, and each plane had a little piano bar up a small flight of stairs above the tail section. On this particular flight, there were two bands of musicians flirting and joking with a group of pretty young stewardesses who were serving cocktails. This volatile combination was a surefire recipe for trouble.

Thanks to the superb service of the fine stewardesses, the musicians got just a little bombed. Then both bands retired to the piano bar for an impromptu rock & roll jam session that included two piano players, vocalists, and rock & roll wannabes from among the rest of the passengers. Man, the plane was rocking and rolling all the way out to L.A., much to the dismay of the crew and the other passengers. Not surprisingly, the next time I flew on a 747 there was no piano bar, just regular seats above the tail section.

We arrived at a hotel in L.A., on the Sunset Strip, called the Continental Hyatt House. It was nicknamed "The Zoo" because in the early seventies a lot of strange people hung out there. The following day we went to the TV studio and appeared on *Soul Train*. The place was really jammed with exuberant kids doing their thing in front of the cameras. The audience really gave us a rousing reception when we went into "Scorpio." We were inspired by their enthusiasm, so we played really hot and funky. I wondered why the studio was so crowded and found out later that when they announced that we would be on the show the turnout was 40 percent more than usual. They videotaped the show that day and showed it again later that year.

Later that year I bumped into Don Cornelius at the bar in the Hyatt Regency after I had just gotten married. My new wife Kathy and I were looking for a house out in L.A. Don congratulated us and sent a bottle of champagne to our table. To me, that was real class, and I never forgot it.

We also had a chance to appear on *American Bandstand* with Dick Clark, which I used to watch as a teenager when it was still in Philadelphia. In fact, someone from my graduating class at Mackenzie High in Detroit wrote in my high school yearbook, "See ya on *American Bandstand*. Good luck!" Little did he know . . .

I recall that weekend very vividly because it was the same weekend I performed at a concert in Washington, D.C., with Donny Hathaway and Les McCann. After the concert was over on Friday night, I took the redeye flight out to L.A. to be on time for the show Saturday morning.

On the show, we pantomimed to "Scorpio," and that was our performance. Again, the audience was very responsive, so they videotaped the show and it was played once more at a later date.

When the show was over, back at the hotel, I got a frantic call from Carol, my live-in baby-sitter. My three kids were out of control and going wild, so she asked me to please come home and settle them down.

When I got home, I was not a happy camper. In the same weekend, I had flown from Detroit to Washington, D.C., to L.A. and then back to Detroit. I did give out a few spankings that day, but I realized that without a mother my kids felt insecure and would get upset whenever I went on the road. In the future, I decided I'd travel as little as possible.

For a guest shot on the *Mike Douglas Show* in Philadelphia, I went into the studio a week before the show and mixed down "Scorpio" without the lead melody so I could play live on the show with the band track. I probably should have used the TV studio band for backup, but I needed congas and percussion for the breakdown and I needed Bob Babbitt to play that outrageous bass solo.

On the day of the show, I flew to Philadelphia, and Mike interviewed me briefly. When it was over, I said goodbye to him and his twenty million viewers. And that was it. Welcome to big-time show business.

They taped the show that day, and scheduled it for viewing in about two weeks. On the day of the show, I was staying at my cottage on Stag Island, in Canada, in the middle of the St. Clair River north of Detroit. I convinced my mother-in-law to ask a neighbor on the island to let us watch his TV because he owned the only color TV on the island. She didn't bother to tell him why we wanted to watch.

That day we sat in his living room as he fiddled around with the various adjustments, making sure we had a good picture. Finally, in the last segment of the show, I was introduced and began playing "Scorpio." As he watched the show, the old guy's eyes got as big as saucers. He shook his head back and forth and did a double take. He looked at me, and then he looked at the TV set. He looked at me again, and then he looked at the TV set. Finally, he shook his finger in my face.

"Hey," he sputtered, "that's you on that set. But you're sitting right here. How in the hell can that be? Ol' Mike's got him a live show, don't he?"

I had to explain that they videotape live talk shows in front of a small studio audience and then show them whenever they want. "I taped that particular show in Philadelphia over two weeks ago," I said.

The old guy looked at me, shook his head, and muttered something under his breath that I couldn't hear.

As we left, I turned to my mother-in-law and said, "I'm sure talk shows will never be the same for him again."

California Dreamin'

In 1972, I met and married my second wife, Kathy. In 1973, I gave up the road and made the decision to sell the house and move my family to L.A. The only major record company in Detroit was Motown, but there was no evidence of growth or expansion over on the Boulevard. Actually, just the opposite was happening; most of the Motown sessions were now being recorded at Motown Studios West off Santa Monica Boulevard in L.A.

I convinced my partner, Mike Theodore, that if we were going to stay in the record business we would have to relocate to California. The music business was really booming out there.

Back in those days, it seemed like everything I touched turned to gold, so I wasn't too concerned about relocating. I had hits on the national charts and plenty of money coming in from playing guitar. I was also writing, producing, and arranging, so my bank account had grown substantially.

On one of my prior visits to L.A., I had gone shopping with the rich and famous at Giorgio's on Rodeo Drive in Beverly Hills. Sussex Records' promotion man, Chuck Fassert, had taken me there to get two new suits—one to wear at my wedding and one to wear on *The Mike Douglas Show*. At the time, I had a record that was number six on *Billboard's* national pop chart, so I guess that made me a star.

Chuck really made a big deal of it to the people at Giorgio's, so they gave me the red carpet treatment.

After we walked inside, Chuck introduced me to the manager, who called over this tantalizing brunette. She was very conservatively dressed, but even so the outfit couldn't hide her curvy body.

"Can I get you a drink?" she purred as she floated over, looking like an advertisement for "Legs 'R Us."

"Excuse me?" I said. I'd never heard of anyone getting served a drink at a clothing store.

"Would you like something to drink?" she said.

"What do you have?"

"Whatever you like," she said with a coy smile, flipping a lush, full mane of brown hair away from her face.

"Well then," I replied jokingly, "bring me a scotch and water."

I almost fell over when she really brought me a scotch and water.

A few drinks and twelve hundred dollars later, I was the proud owner of two brand new suits. It was a good thing I'd had a few belts of booze to lessen the pain because it was about eight hundred dollars more than I would normally have spent.

Maybe that was part of their marketing strategy or maybe the rich and famous of Beverly Hills and Bel Air had so much money they didn't really care how much they spent as long as someone catered to their every whim. I was still the new kid on the block and didn't have a clue.

To Giorgio's credit, the two suits were very unique. One was blue and white and made of soft tanned leather. The other was brown crushed velvet. When I got home to Detroit, I noticed that the Giorgio label on the inside of both jacket collars was upside down. I thought it was a mistake until someone told me they were made that way on purpose, so if you were at a party and placed your coat over a chair everyone could read the label. I don't know if I believed that or not, but in Hollywood, where image is everything, anything seemed possible.

Kathy and I flew out to L.A. to find a house, and when Chuck Fassert, the Sussex record promotion man, suggested I look in the San Fernando Valley, that's where I began my search. When you tell someone from the business community in L.A. that you're in the music business, they treat you like royalty. In Detroit, when you tell a banker or real estate agent that you're a musician, they treat you like a lowlife.

We eventually found a house we liked in Canoga Park, adjacent to Woodland Hills, at the far end of the valley. It was a magnificent, five-bedroom, white stucco house with a beautiful, spacious backyard just perfect for entertaining. There was a forty-two foot lighted pool and a high cement block wall for privacy surrounding the entire yard. I could see mountains in the background over the far wall on the other side of the pool. Of course, I discovered later that when we had a smog alert in the summer the mountains became a yellow haze floating in the air and stayed that way until a blast from the Santa Anna desert winds cleared out the valley.

The yard had a patio with a roof and a gas barbecue next to a small square of heated stones, where you could sit after a swim in the chilly night air. It also had a heater in the pool in case the water got too cold at night. The living room had a big orange-brick fireplace with gas-fired artificial logs. At first, I didn't understand the reason for a fireplace in California, but after a few chilly desert nights I did.

Kathy and I decided that this was the house for us, so I made a bid on it and then we went back to our hotel on Hollywood Boulevard to wait nervously and see if it would be accepted. When it finally was, we went out for dinner at a Mexican restaurant, drank a lot of margaritas, and celebrated for the remainder of the night. The next day we drove out to the real estate office in the valley and signed the papers. Then we flew back to Detroit to tell my kids, Jordan, Denise, and Dennis, that we were moving to Los Angeles.

Life in the Valley

Los Angeles, 1973

Our move to California turned out to be a major undertaking. We had so much stuff to move that we had to hire a moving company to help us pack before they even loaded up the truck.

The drive to California took about four days of hard, serious driving, and we stopped each night at a motel and rested.

The day we finally drove through the San Bernardino Mountains, approaching L.A., I felt slightly intimidated, driving down the massive ten-lane freeway jammed with cars, trucks, and everything else on wheels belching fire and brimstone. I wasn't used to driving on a freeway with so many lanes, especially one that was so unbelievably crowded, with angry drivers all honking their horns at once. Of course, they could honk all they wanted because most of the time the traffic didn't move. Welcome to Los Angeles.

Once we were settled in our house, I began to live the life of the rich and famous. I became a legend in my own mind. Success in show business can do that to you. I had almost everything I wanted and all the trappings of wealth and status that most people only imagine. Never in my wildest dreams had I expected any of this.

I hired people to do jobs around the house. I had a local family come out once a week to do my gardening, somebody to take care of my pool, and a cleaning lady on a regular basis. Kathy and I went out for dinner once or twice a week, and we blew money like crazy. I traded in my Cadillac Fleetwood Brougham and bought a yellow 280C Mercedes coupe.

After we unpacked, I went to see Clarence Avant at Sussex, the record label that had me under contract, and then I called the folks at Motown to tell them I was out here as well. I really didn't know anyone else in L.A., so now the waiting game began. I sat by my pool day after day and listened for the telephone to ring. I had a job as a staff record producer with Sussex, but I still relied on recording sessions to pay the bills. Living in the valley was not an inexpensive proposition then and probably isn't now.

After two months of moping around the house, I settled down by the pool and tried to look relaxed as I got some sun. The only sound that greeted me each day as I stared at the phone was an eerie silence. I began to feel paranoid, and I wondered if I had made the wrong decision about moving out here. I was beginning to spend the majority of my time floating around in the pool in my rubber raft with a drink in my hand, playing the role of an L.A. big shot. I was waiting for someone to call and offer me a recording session in one of the most competitive entertainment cities in the world.

Suddenly, to my surprise, the telephone really did ring. I climbed out of the pool and picked up the receiver. I heard a sweet voice reaching out to touch someone on the other end of the line.

"This is Sharon from Your Girl calling for Ben Barrett, the contractor for Motown Records."

Who the hell was "your girl"? I wondered to myself.

"Are you available to do a session next Thursday at ten o'clock?"

When I heard the magic word, my ears perked up like a racehorse put out to pasture getting saddled up for one more race.

The recording scene in L.A. was very different from the one I was used to in Detroit. When I first worked at Motown in Detroit, Hank Cosby was the Motown contractor. Later Ernest Kelly held down the position. In L.A., the contractors were independent and worked for many different companies. They usually had assistants, and everyone used an answering service to coordinate their recording schedules. That's how busy things were. It got so hectic at times that I'd get a contractor's answering service patched through to my answering service patched through to me for verification of a hot session that was coming up in the next few days.

Contractors were usually paid double scale, but as long as each session started on time and everyone showed up the contractor didn't have to stay too long. Each contractor had more than one session going on at the same time. The contractors were the true power brokers on the L.A. music scene. If you got any of them mad at you and got a bad rep, you were out of the session business.

Another interesting thing about the L.A. scene was the configuration of the recording studios. They didn't have guitar amplifiers or speaker boxes to play your instrument through like in Detroit. In L.A., you had to bring your own amplifier, which led to the emergence of cartage industries that transported your equipment from studio to studio.

MoWest in L.A. was quite a contrast to the old Hitsville studios on Grand Boulevard in Detroit. MoWest was in a new, two-story brick building that resembled an office complex. The new building had two main recording studios, one upstairs and one downstairs. It also had an atrium with plants surrounded by chairs and a table sitting in an open courtyard right in the middle of the building.

One day, after I had been there a while, I looked around me in the studio and noticed bits and pieces of the old Motown studio back in Detroit. I saw a drum baffle, a sound separator, and a familiar microphone or two sitting in a corner, and I wondered why Motown had moved all that stuff to L.A. It felt really strange seeing it here, three thousand miles from home in sunny California, where almost everything else was brand new and unfamiliar.

When I arrived at MoWest and walked down the hall toward one of the studios, the first person I saw was Smokey Robinson. I waved at Smokey as he passed me in the hall and he waved back. I was beginning to feel more comfortable already. I saw a few other people I recognized, but studio musicians are sometimes like the shop rats who work the automotive production lines in Detroit. The big bosses very rarely came down to the line or the studio where the work was actually being done, so the people we saw the most were musicians like ourselves and arrangers and producers.

In the seven years I worked at Motown, I saw Berry Gordy in the studio only twice, and both times he had Diana Ross in tow. The first time we were at Hitsville, recording a Supremes tune called "I'm Living In Shame." On this song, there were two breakdowns, and because I had a lot of freedom to try out my ideas on the sessions I decided to play guitar feedback. I had to turn up the volume on my guitar extremely loud to produce feedback through the Fender amplifier I had brought to the studio. I had to sit in the overdub room to keep the sound of my guitar from leaking onto the other instrument tracks. At Motown, we recorded each song on a twenty-four-track tape recorder with a different instrument or voice on each track. After we completed the song, the sounds from the twenty-four tracks were mixed down into two-track stereo.

That day, I was sitting in a chair in the overdub room, playing my crazy feedback stuff on the tune, when I glanced up and saw Berry Gordy and Diana Ross peering through the window behind me.

I could tell by the look on their faces that Berry and Diana probably wondered why this crazy guitar player was making all that noise in the overdub room. Berry looked back over his shoulder and asked someone behind him what was going on. I didn't hear the answer.

On my first visit to MoWest, I started recording tracks in Studio A at 10:00 A.M. Monday morning. I didn't leave the studio until 4:00 A.M. the following day. Every time I finished cutting rhythm tracks in Studio A, they would send me to Studio B upstairs to do guitar overdubs until the next rhythm session began in Studio A. Then I'd go down to Studio A and repeat the sequence all over again. I sure made a lot of money that day and enjoyed every minute of it. The only thing missing was the Motown Cats from Detroit. If Motown had brought the entire "A Team" from Detroit out to L.A., they would have recorded so many hits that even the record executives out there would have been impressed.

One of the first sessions I did at Motown West was a guitar overdub on a song by the Miracles (minus Smokey) called "Do It Baby." I overdubbed a funky low guitar part to the record in the style known in Detroit as "chicken pickin'." The record was released in a few months, moved right up the national charts, and became a hit. "Do It Baby" was one of the first hits I played on in L.A. and one of the few hits the Miracles had without Smokey singing lead.

Some of the musicians I worked with at MoWest were Ed Green and James Gadson on drums, Wilton Felder on bass, and Joe Sample on keyboards, the latter two members of the Crusaders. Jay Graydon, Wah Wah Watson, Arthur Adams, and I provided the guitar. Except for Wah Wah, who wasn't there that much, the musical feel was a lot different from what I was used to playing at Hitsville. Although the L.A. musicians were great, Motown didn't have access to the same players each day because they were already booked or on the road. Ben Barrett, the Motown contractor, had a pool of musicians he called, and he scheduled the ones who were available. After playing sessions at MoWest for a few months, I finally realized that the Motown Sound really was lost and gone forever.

What I really missed the most at MoWest was the hard, funky groove that was born and bred on the urban streets of the Motor City. It was as much a part of me then as it is now. It's an intense way of playing music that comes from way down deep inside your soul. The sound of the Motor City reflects the raw experiences of life, and it saturates your very being and stays with you forever. It is probably the reason why I always came back to Detroit and why I'm here now.

One of the Motown artists who did come to the studio was Marvin Gaye. When I heard about his tragic death after I moved back to Detroit in 1976, I remembered the last time I worked with him at MoWest. It was very late on a balmy summer night, and we were in the studio recording one of Marvin's songs. He was with us in the studio, directing us toward the music he heard inside of his head.

Marvin was really laid-back that night, wearing jeans, a T-shirt, and a light jacket. As we played the music and read the charts, he wandered back and forth in front of us, adding a soft comment here and there. That day stood out in my mind because Marvin was smoking a joint in the studio for most of the session.

The entire time I did sessions at Motown, I never saw anyone smoking a joint in the studio or during a take, but that was Marvin. He was a laid-back, easygoing kind of guy. He was a very deep person with a lot of creativity and soul, and I was surprised and saddened to hear of his death at the hands of his own father.

On another late session at MoWest, Diana Ross was producing. Berry Gordy was at her side that night as she walked around the room from time to time, giving us suggestions. Diana was very soft-spoken and appeared fragile and delicate. As I concentrated on the music, it was difficult for me to remember that she was such a huge superstar. We completed the session, and I looked forward to my next call. I never knew what I would be expected to play or who I might see.

L.A. Superstars

One of the strangest jobs I had in L.A. was enough to give a serious musician nightmares or a nonserious musician a few hysterical belly laughs. On this particular night, Motown asked me to back up the newest singer in their stable, a high-energy performer from Detroit named Mike Campbell. I had known Mike ever since I wrote the arrangements for his first record contract for RCA with Ray Monette, his partner, who eventually became the guitarist for the group Rare Earth. The Motown job was at the Troubadour, a folk club in L.A.

The Troubadour was a large club, and I'd been there a few times before. It was where I saw Bill Withers and the Pointer Sisters when they first started as well as Chick Corea's jazz fusion group Return to Forever.

That night I knew I was in trouble when someone from Motown came out and insisted we put on these loud "Desi Arnez" type Cuban shirts, with open collars and puffy white sleeves. We were professionals, so we did as we were told. After I put on the shirt and looked at myself in the mirror, I was beginning to feel a little stupid, but, as the saying goes, "The show must go on."

I was playing with so much enthusiasm that Berry Gordy Sr., who at the time resembled Colonel Sanders, with his white hair, goatee, and cane, sent me a note and asked me to turn my amplifier down. Of

course, I would have been a damn fool to ignore a request by Berry
Gordy's father, who appeared to be backing the show, so I did as I
was told and turned it down.

Just before the finale of the show, Mike Campbell publicly
thanked Berry Gordy Sr. and Motown for making his show business
debut possible. Then Mike left the stage, and we started vamping the
chords for the last tune of the set, an oldie called "Chapel of Love."

Mike Campbell suddenly waltzed onstage, to a collective gasp
from the audience, and belted out his favorite melody. I gasped
myself when I saw what he was wearing. He had changed into a stun-
ning white wedding gown, complete with veil and flowers, and he
was swaying to the music and singing: "Gonna get marrieeed, gonna
get marrieeed, gonna get marrieeed, in the chapel of love." Mike's
two female backup singers appeared on either side of him, dutifully
singing the appropriate doo-wops, only now they were wearing big
banana costumes, which made them look like they were straddling
two six-foot-long canoes.

As the girls moved back and forth to the music, each banana,
which probably had been a canoe in a past life, swayed back and
forth, menacing the spectators in the front row. I actually felt sorry
for Berry Gordy Sr., who, after that magnificent introduction, looked
like he wanted to crawl under the table.

Well, I thought to myself, through all the laughter and snickering
coming from the audience, things could be a lot worse. And sure
enough I was about to see just how bad things could be.

I had just gotten over the shock of a man in a wedding gown and
two girls dressed like bananas when I had another. Mike lifted up the
voluminous folds of his gown and a male midget in a strapless
evening gown jumped out, dancing furiously to the music.

It was a good thing I was sitting on a stool, because I was laughing so hard that if I'd been standing I probably would have fallen
down. I could barely glimpse Berry Gordy Sr. in the audience, but he
sure didn't look very happy, judging by the scowl he now had on his
face. I shook my head a few times, wondering if this entire fiasco was
one huge nightmare and if I was really at home asleep in my own
bed. Here I was playing with some of the finest studio musicians in
L.A., backing up a wacko in a wedding gown, accompanied by two

other wackos in banana outfits and one in a strapless evening gown. Holy Superman and Batman cartoons, this couldn't be real, I had to be dreaming!

After the show was over, I packed up my gear and slunk out of the club. When I got home, I had a couple of martinis to numb my brain as I wondered why the hell I had come out here. I didn't have an answer.

Later Mike became known as Mike Champion, a successful actor on TV and in feature films with Clint Eastwood and other major stars. It was a good career move for Mike because I had the distinct feeling that his singing career with Motown went down the toilet that day.

I learned early on that L.A. is a town of contrasts and ironies, and fortunately a year after my experience with Mike Campbell I had a chance to play with Barbra Streisand. She renewed my faith in the true meaning of the word *artist*.

It all began when I got a call from a keyboardist friend of mine. I had used him on a few sessions, and he was now returning the favor. He said Barbra would be performing in Century City for a group of Columbia bigwigs and all their worldwide distributors. Because of her high status, there would be a sixty-piece orchestra accompanying her, including an entire horn and string section. We would be rehearsing with her the day of the concert at the CBS Recording Studio. When I hung up the phone, I could hardly wait to play the gig.

When the day finally arrived, I went to the studio and was totally awed by the size of the orchestra. There were violins, violas, cellos, trumpets, trombones, saxophones, and a complete rhythm section, including percussion. This would be almost like playing with a full symphony orchestra.

Barbra had a lunch buffet catered in for all the musicians, and as we walked by and filled up our plates she stood at the head of the line and greeted everyone. I had seen her before in movies, but seeing her in person that day I felt that the big screen didn't really do her justice. In person, she was absolutely beautiful! She looked like musical royalty that day and carried herself like the superstar she was.

Marty Paige conducted the orchestra at the rehearsal that day. Marty was a well-known arranger and also the father of David Paige, a fellow session buddy and also the piano player for the group Toto. We had a great time playing the music, and everything ran smoothly, including working with Barbra. She was very friendly and gracious to us, and I felt that a lot of the stories I'd read about her being temperamental and hard to work with were probably unfounded.

The night of the concert, I could feel electricity crackling in the air. The room was small and intimate compared to the big concert halls Barbra was probably used to. Chairs and tables surrounded the small stage. The organization of the event was impressive. When I arrived, the place was already packed, standing room only. Security was tighter than at a presidential primary. We were issued blue badges to get backstage and setup our equipment. Barbra did a sound check before the show, which was interrupted by a nasty squeal of feedback from the sound system. She got a little testy and chewed out the sound technician, but I couldn't blame her for that.

During the concert, I was playing my acoustic guitar behind Barbra's performance on the beautiful song "The Way We Were," with the lush orchestra playing harmoniously in the background, when I heard the sound that every guitar player learns to dread. SNAP! It was the sound of one my guitar strings breaking in half as it wrapped itself behind the neck of my guitar.

As an experienced professional, I did what I always did in situations like that. I played on the other five strings without missing a note. I don't believe anyone else was aware that I had broken a string. As soon as the song was over, I went back to using my electric guitar and that was that—on with the show.

The most impressive part of the show was Barbra herself. She was mesmerizing and totally awesome, the consummate artist, holding the appreciative audience in the palm of her hand. She sang beautifully and showed so much power and emotion in her voice that it gave me the chills. From wedding gowns, midget clowns, and banana costumes to this. The contrast was amazing—only in California.

Another L.A. recording session I had the pleasure of working was equally impressive but from another perspective. This time I had the opportunity to work with Ringo Starr.

The first time I met Ringo we just nodded and said hello as I set up my equipment and unpacked my guitar in the recording studio. Ringo seemed like a real nice guy. We had two drummers on the session, just like we'd always had in Detroit.

The other drummer was a fine player named Jim Keltner. I had met Jim before on other sessions in L.A. Jim played drums with a real laid-back, pop feel and had previously recorded with well-known pop stars such as John Lennon and Carly Simon. This type of session was a little different for me because I was used to the hard groove of the Funk Brothers back in Detroit. I had played on pop hits before but with the Royaltones and Del Shannon.

The bass player on the session was Klaus Voorman from Germany. The keyboard player was New Orleans funkster Dr. John. We were a pretty diverse and experienced group of studio musicians. The producer was Richard Perry, who produced a lot of acts, including Carly Simon and the Pointer Sisters. Richard was the original laid back record producer and was always asking for one more take. We could take three hours plus per song, and Richard would still ask for just one more take. Later I heard that when the session was finished Richard would select the best verses from each take of the song and splice them together to make one great take. He was the only producer I knew who used that technique.

L.A. in the seventies was a place that always had a lot of substances around to abuse. Some recording artists and producers, with unlimited money and attitudes dating back to the drug culture of the sixties, did whatever they pleased whenever they pleased.

At the beginning of the recording session with Richard Perry, there was free beer, wine, marijuana, and fruit and cheese on a hospitality table. After recording for six or eight hours straight at four in the morning, the musicians were feeling a little tired and run down.

Finally, it was time to record the last few takes and time also to open up your sinuses and free your mind—or blow your nose or your mind. For that, we had the most popular recreational drug in vogue at the time, King Cocaine! Cocaine certainly got everyone up to play some extra takes without complaining. Of course, we wanted to play each song a little faster than usual. Well, maybe a lot faster than usual. Or maybe it just felt like we were playing a lot faster than usual. We had reached the point where nobody knew. After we had played back-to-back sessions all day and most of the night, who in the hell cared?

Finally, at about four in the morning, Richard called it a wrap, and we went on home. Talk about being wasted. My ass was draggin' big time. I started up my yellow Mercedes 280C, entered the Hollywood Freeway, and drove home out in the valley. I crashed in my bed and went to sleep at about 5:00 A.M. Of course, my wife Kathy yelled at me for hanging out, but it was a righteous good-paying gig. At least I was getting paid big money to play music and hang out with my friends.

After the long recording session with Ringo, I decided to take a well-deserved break. I was getting homesick for the wide open spaces of Upper Michigan, so I hired a guide and took a hunting trip on horseback in the High Sierras. There I learned a lot about cowboys and how bad horses can smell when they're out climbing mountains all day, especially if you sleep under the stars using a saddle as a pillow. I also learned that chasing mule deer out of rifle range from one mountain to another was not a good way to bag one.

After four days in the bush, we got back to base camp, and there was a message for me. Here I was, ten thousand feet up in the High Sierras, and Richard Perry's office in Hollywood calls and leaves a message that Ringo needs me for another session. Even up here in the wild California mountains, it was still show business as usual. The next day, after I arrived back home, I went directly to the studio to continue my work on the *Goodnight Vienna* album.

Richard Perry was late, so while we waited I regaled Ringo with stories of my recent hunting expedition up in the High Sierras. If I was boring him, he was polite enough not to let on. We talked for half an hour, and I learned that Ringo was a real friendly guy. He didn't mention his career or the Beatles much. He was probably all talked out on that subject already, and I didn't ask. Eventually, Richard Perry drove up in his shiny, black Bentley. He walked into the studio dressed like a farmer in his bib overalls. I got my guitar out, and we completed the session.

Dennis and partner Mike Theodore. (Photo courtesy of Mike Theodore.)

Dennis at the age of thirteen, his sister Pat, and his first electric guitar. (Photo courtesy of Gertrude Schultz.)

The Pyramids playing at the Top Hat teen club. *Left to right:* Dennis, Bob Gursky, Jim "Mouse" Pascot, Orin Rosenblat, and Val Gursky. (Photo courtesy of Sean Gursky and Val Gursky.)

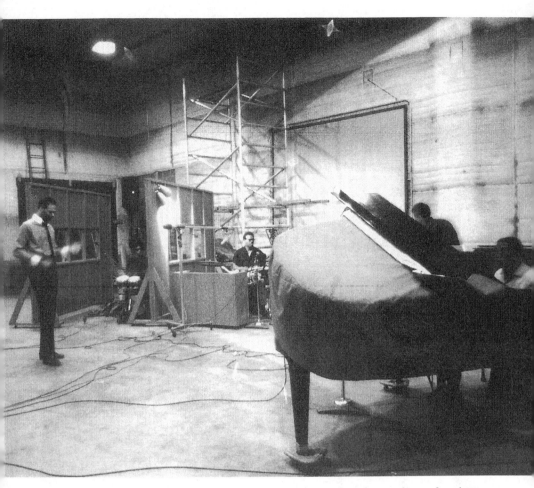

The "Got to Pay the Price" session at United Sound Studios. *Left to right:* Al Kent, Bobbie Hall, Uriel Jones, unidentified, and Joe Hunter. (Photo courtesy of Ed Wolfrum.)

Recording session at BA Star Studio in Detroit. *Left to right:* Don Davis, Bob Babbitt, Dennis. (Photo courtesy of Ed Wolfrum.)

Eddie Willis and Dennis at a recording session at United Sound Studios. (Photo courtesy of Ed Wolfrum.)

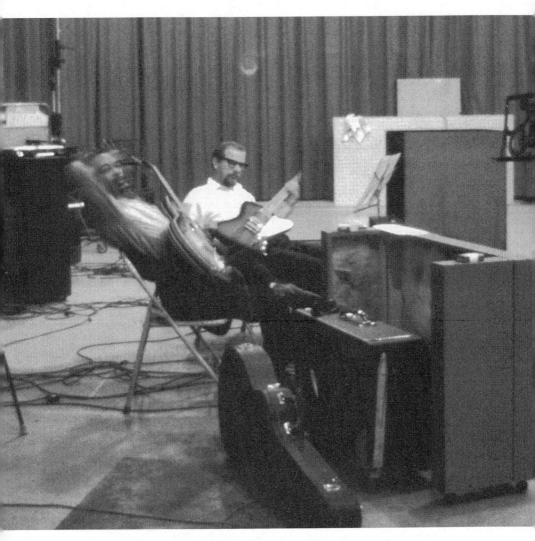

Eddie Willis and Dennis at the "Got to Pay the Price" recording session. (Photo courtesy of Ed Wolfrum.)

Dennis Coffey album cover. (Courtesy of Clarence Avant.)

Dennis's Motown ID card

Cover of *Cash Box* magazine featuring Bill Withers, the Gallery, and Dennis

The Detroit Guitar Band. *Left to right:* Bob Babbitt, Eric Morgenson, Andrew Smith, Dennis, and James Barnes. (Photo by the author.)

Party at Gary Dean's house. *Left to right, standing:* Bob Babbitt,
Motown Funk Brothers bass; Mike Terry, Motown sax player and
arranger; John Trudell, Motown trumpet player; Richard "Pistol"
Allen, Motown Funk Brothers drums; Dennis; Rodney Knight, singer.
Seated: Uriel Jones, Motown Funk Brothers drums; Gary Dean, singer.
Standing in front of Dennis: Buddy Budson, keyboards and arranger.
(Photo courtesy of Gary Dean Salisbury.)

Dennis and Motown Funk Brothers upstairs at Hitsville during the filming of
Standing in the Shadows of Motown. Left to right: Joe Messina, Motown Funk
Brothers guitar; Dennis; Bob Babbitt, Motown Funk Brothers bass; and Johnny
Griffith, Motown Funk Brothers keyboards. (Photo courtesy of Craig Weiland.)

Motown and Ric-Tic singer Edwin Starr and Dennis at the Benedum Theater in Philadelphia during the taping of the PBS special *Rhythm, Love and Soul.* (Photo courtesy of Harry Weinger.)

Dennis and George Katsakis, the Royaltones' sax player. (Photo courtesy of Gary Dean Salisbury.)

Dennis's son, produc and drummer James Coffey, with Motowr trumpet player John Trudell. (Photo courtesy of Gary De Salisbury.)

Movies and Television

O ne reason why I went out to L.A. was to explore a career in the movie and TV business. I'd always wondered what it would be like to write music for a film or a TV show. Well, I was never accused of being shy, so I got Clarence Avant to talk to Ed Silverman at Warner Brothers Music, who had just released a guitar book of my songs. Warner Brothers hooked me up with Fred Wientraub, a film producer who was completing a movie called *Black Belt Jones*.

Black Belt Jones was the legacy of martial arts legend Bruce Lee and featured a young, African American karate star named Jim Kelly. Most of the film scoring was already completed, but they still needed a main theme and a love theme to add commercial flavor to the music, and they were hoping for a hit.

On my first visit to the Warner Brothers lot, I found myself in the actual location where many of the greatest movies of all time had been filmed. The Warner Brothers lot included two-story buildings used as soundstages and streets and buildings used for location shots. There was a guardhouse with a lift gate blocking the driveway at the front entrance, and you needed a pass to get in. I was running a little late so I entered the lot and grabbed the first open parking spot I saw. Later I had to go out and move my car because David Jansen, the star of *The Fugitive*, needed his parking spot for his shiny black Rolls Royce sedan with tinted windows. Well, excuuuse me!

I was meeting Fred Wientraub, the man responsible for producing Bruce Lee's high-action, high-camp karate films in the seventies. Fred was a chubby, fast-talking chain smoker and wore a goatee. He gave me a copy of the script and explained what he wanted. He showed me some scenes from the film to give me an idea of what he was talking about. I asked him a few questions about the music and suggested that we use voices like lead instruments singing without lyrics. Fred thought that was a great idea. I went home to write the music.

Looking over the script at home, I discovered that all the scenes and dialogue were timed right down to the second. The tempo of the songs had to be exact, which was why movie and TV music was always recorded to a click track on the tape. Each click represented a beat and was synchronized to a time code on the film. The click track could be changed to fit the speed of the song, but once the tempo was set the musicians had to play to the beat of the clicks.

I sat down at home and got out my guitar and wrote the main theme and the love theme. When I finished, I called my partner Mike Theodore and we wrote snappy horn and string arrangements and made plans to go into the recording studio. I was always looking for something new, so I decided to write a four-part counterpoint vocal arrangement and record the voices singing through my wah-wah pedal. To my knowledge, this had never been done before, so I couldn't wait to see what it would sound like and if it would work.

Finally, the big day arrived and the film was completed. I was invited, along with Kathy, to Warner Brothers for a preview in one of their screening rooms. At the beginning of the film, as the credits rolled by, I noticed that they had misspelled my name: "Coffy." I also noticed that the music sounded a little muffled, while all the karate kicks and slaps came out loud and clear. The dialogue was also loud and crisp, and it dawned on me that the producers didn't really care that much about the quality of the music. I made a vow to myself that day that until I could work with a film producer who really believed music would enhance his production I wouldn't do any more of them.

One day, I received a call from Ben Barrett, Motown's musical contractor. I got along well with Ben, and because Motown always paid me time and a half of scale for each recording session, I had plenty of reasons to get along with everybody at Motown Studios West. Time and a half came out to about forty-five dollars per hour—great money in the seventies. Actually, it would be great money even now, in spite of inflation.

I could tell by the tone of his voice that something really big was in the wind.

"It's Michael Jackson and the Jackson Five," Ben said nonchalantly. "They need you to back them up in a live concert at the Century Plaza Hotel for all the Motown distributors across the country. They'll also have a complete horn section."

I told him it sounded great. "When do I get to rehearse?"

A little sheepishly, Ben told me they'd already had the last rehearsal.

"You mean to tell me," I exploded over the telephone, "that I don't even get to rehearse? You expect me to read their music charts cold? And try not to shoot myself in the foot in front of all those record business big shots! I don't think so! On top of that," I said, "my wife and I just had a baby and my in-laws are in town this weekend, expecting me to entertain them. I told them I had the weekend off. Man, I really don't want to do this. Can't you find someone else?"

"The Jackson Five and Motown requested you!" Ben countered firmly. "They don't want anyone else."

Ben went into a show business power trip as he applied the pressure.

"You know, you're on almost all of our sessions," he reasoned, "and we pay you scale and a half. If you refuse, there'll be trouble. Motown isn't bluffing. They're bent out of shape over this one. One of their hottest acts in the country is in a jam. Motown would take it very seriously if you didn't help them out. And I would probably forget your phone number for all the non-Motown sessions and TV calls I contract as well. I'd really think this over for about half a minute because that's all the time you have to make up your mind," he said.

In the past, I would have stood my ground. Now I was a little older and a little wiser, and this time I felt Ben and Motown weren't just blowing smoke. I was silent for about fifteen seconds, and then I made my decision.

"OK," I finally answered, "I'll do it. But I have to take my in-laws to the show. I promised I'd entertain them this weekend before they go back to Detroit."

That Saturday night I arrived at the Century Plaza with my in-laws. My father-in-law, Harry Osborn, was a retired Detroit cop. He and his wife Kelly were friendly and outgoing. I made sure they were seated before I made my way up to the bandstand. As I set up, the bandleader walked over to me, introduced himself, and gave me the music book.

When I looked the music over, I realized that this was not going to be an easy book to read. It was kind of funny because the week before I was at the same place, backing up Barbra Streisand with a sixty-piece orchestra, and we rehearsed our parts all day long before the show that night. Now, I was getting ready to play a show, equally as complicated, with no rehearsal whatsoever. I also noticed a long, four-page medley of songs from the forties, including clarinetist Benny Goodman's "Sing, Sing, Sing." I had a feeling it was going to be a long night.

Once the show began, I played the charts as written and didn't lose my place. I tried very hard not to embarrass myself. I don't think their drummer knew of my history with Motown because he kept glaring at me throughout the show. Maybe he was good friends with the former guitar player or he didn't like what I was playing. For me, it was a very ticklish situation. I had to improvise and read the music just to get through the show in one piece. I was beginning to feel just a little bit used and abused. I waited until a real juicy guitar part came up, one that allowed me to stretch out a bit, turned my amplifier way up, and in true Coffey style "let 'er rip." What the hell. As many Motown hits as I had played on, I figured I was entitled to strut my stuff a little bit. I was in the drummer's face and jamming.

During the finale of the show, a pretty little girl named Janet, around seven or eight years old, was escorted onto the stage wearing a green gown with a big bow tied in the back. She sang a song with the Jackson Five. The crowd went wild. Even at that age, she had stage presence and knew how to smile and tug at the heartstrings of an audience. The Jackson family sure believed in starting them young.

When the show was over, I thought about Janet Jackson, who was singing and entertaining a grownup audience, and I remembered the day at Golden World when I brought my daughter Jordan to the studio because I was stuck for a baby-sitter. I was always real careful how much I exposed my children to the world of show business.

At the time, I looked at show business families like the Osmonds and the Jacksons and saw other grownup child stars on TV complaining of being dropped from hit shows when they outgrew their cuteness. I wondered if they ever got the chance to enjoy their childhood. I think traveling on the road or working a grownup job in a movie or TV studio robs a child of the most important and wondrous years of his or her life. Those are the years when children find their own identities, which may or may not match the lives that their parents have envisioned for them.

I recorded an album in L.A. for Capital Records with the Osmonds. Members of the Osmonds were in the recording studio during the session, but they pretty much sat and watched on the sidelines while we worked with the producer and arranger to record the music for their band tracks. When their album was released, I was surprised to see the Osmonds getting all the credit on the back of the album for playing each instrument. As far as I knew, they didn't play at all—we did!

My kids were just not real show business types. I felt bad moving them from Detroit to L.A. and then to New York so I could make a living in the studio. At least I was home and not on the road for months at a time. We always lived in nice neighborhoods, and my kids always had a lot of friends to play with. We also had our cottage on Stag Island, so they had a place to come home to even when we lived out of state.

I entered the music business because that was my choice, not because my family wanted me to. If my family had forced me into the business as a teenager, I would have really been resentful when my own personal crash and burn came in 1985 and I found myself out of work. Instead, when I did crash I blamed myself and the record business. The record business is fickle and chews up artists and spits them out when the next musical fad comes along.

Not long after the completion of *Black Belt Jones* and the Jackson Five concert, Mike Theodore and I managed to get into a private club above the old Roxy Theater on the Sunset Strip in Hollywood, and it was there that we learned firsthand that life really can sometimes imitate art.

Mike and I were notorious for gaining entrance to private clubs, whether in New York, Detroit, or L.A. If the club had a DJ or anything to do with music, I'd just ask for the DJ or tell the doorman that the DJ was expecting us. This worked extremely well, especially after we produced "Scorpio."

That night we told the doorman we were successful record producers for Atlantic Records or some other bullshit, and that got us in. We had just sat down at a table when pandemonium broke out on the other side of the club. I looked over and saw this heavily muscled African American man pick up another man and lift him high over his head. Then he spun him like a Frisbee and threw him into the wall, where the guy landed with a sickening thud. The man on the floor appeared to be drunk, but even so he made a wise choice and didn't get up.

"Hey Mike," I yelled. "That's Pinky from the *Black Belt Jones* movie we just did."

Mike agreed and shook his head in disgust.

When things quieted down a bit, I told Mike I was going to go over and say hello.

Mike looked at me as if I'd just taken leave of my senses.

"Are you nuts?! Did you see what he just did to that guy? I wouldn't try talking to him if I were you. You might end up decorating the other wall."

I grinned at Mike and turned in Pinky's direction.

More Movies and Television

O ur visit to the Roxy club on the Sunset Strip was not the first stop we made that night. I was high and feeling no pain, so I walked over to Pinky and introduced myself. "Hey, man. I'm Dennis Coffey. I wrote the music for *Black Belt Jones*. You sure did a great job in the film."

Pinky sat up in his chair and looked at me with a dangerous glint in his eye.

Maybe I did make a mistake walking over here, I thought to myself. I began to feel tense and more than a little apprehensive.

Pinky's face suddenly lit up, and he broke into a wide grin.

"Shit, man, I really dug the music," he said, as he moved a chair away from the table. "Have a seat and let me buy you a drink."

I sat down and had a nice visit with my man, Pinky. After I finished my drink, I walked back over and joined Mike.

"You're lucky he didn't rip your damn face off," he said, shaking his head.

I told Mike he seemed like a pretty nice guy to me.

My last job at Warner Brothers was even stranger than my first. One day I received a call for a record date at the Warner Brothers Recording Studio, which was located in a soundstage on their back lot. I had been at Warner Brothers to do *Black Belt Jones*, but I had never even seen the back lot, where all the movies were made. When

I pulled up, the guard at the gate admitted me and told me how to get to the studio.

I was driving along and following his directions when suddenly things got dark, and there were no streetlights. I was beginning to feel a little nervous, but I turned right anyway, just like it said in the directions. I wasn't all that surprised to discover that I was now at a dead end. Obviously, I'd made a wrong turn somewhere. I turned my car around and drove down the street. I made a left turn, trying to get back on track, and then the strangest thing happened: I looked around and felt like I'd gone back in time. I was lost driving down a street lined with brownstone apartments that looked exactly like New York City circa 1890. The street was cloaked in a weird, misty fog, and I could barely see to drive. Man, this is strange, I said to myself. I made a left turn at the corner, but now I was in Dodge City in the 1800s. Even Wyatt Earp wouldn't be out at this time of night on a street as dark as this.

Now I was really getting rattled. It looked like I would miss the recording session, and I didn't have the faintest idea how to get out. I just kept on driving and driving until I came to an intersection and made another turn. Now I was on a street lined with white picket fences and old spooky mansions and other strange houses, reminding me of the old Dracula and Frankenstein movies. It seemed that every turn I made took me farther and farther into the back lot and each street got progressively darker and scarier.

My imagination started to run wild. I had visions of all the murder mysteries I used to see on old TV shows, where the killer was always some disgruntled actor who had been out of work and living on the movie back lots undetected for years. The killer always managed to find a way to make a stage prop like a sword or a double-edged medieval ax into a real serious weapon.

After endlessly driving around, I made another turn and breathed a huge sigh of relief. In my headlights, I saw a parking lot filled with cars. Musicians were getting out of their cars and carrying their instruments into a large brown building. I looked at my watch and discovered I wasn't even that late.

I was now doing so many sessions in L.A. that I was working with everyone from Tom Jones to Quincy Jones. When I played on Quincy's *Body Heat* album, "Q" walked up to me on the session.

"You know the first time Clarence Avant played me 'Scorpio' I told him it would be a hit," he said. "What a great record."

"Coming from you, Quincy, I'm really flattered," I said. "I appreciate the compliment."

When I worked with Tom Jones in the recording studio, he was exactly the opposite of what I'd expected. Tom drove up to the studio in his Rolls Royce and parked it on the small lot in the back. He walked in through the back door and sat down on the floor in the corner. He sat there during the entire session and didn't say a word to anyone. Considering his explosive stage image, I expected him to come over and introduce himself and tell us what he expected to hear. Maybe he was just worn out from dodging ladies' panties onstage every night. I guess if that happened to me I'd be worn out too.

In the seventies in L.A., the TV industry was also alive and thriving. The first call I got for a TV show was for a new police series called *S.W.A.T.* I was called in to record the main theme and all the dramatic music cues played behind the show. Dramatic cues are used to increase and decrease the tension of the show and to add excitement to the chase scenes. The arranger, composer, and conductor of the show that day was Allyn Ferguson, who had decided to use a sixty-piece orchestra, including horns and strings.

The orchestra recorded the *S.W.A.T.* main theme with Wah Wah Watson, Jay Greydon, and me on guitars. It felt real weird playing with an orchestra while watching a screen on the back wall of the soundstage that showed buildings getting blown up and violent chase scenes. What a strange way to make a living.

When we had finished the main theme to Allyn's satisfaction, we got down to the real grunge work of recording the main music cues. Each music cue appeared on half a page and contained sixteen bars or more, depending on the length of the scene in the show. Each cue was also used to add drama and suspense when something ominous was about to happen or to alert the audience that someone was behaving suspiciously.

Music cues were sometimes difficult to play because quite often there was no definite groove. In fact, to make sure they didn't take attention away from the scene and were the same length as the scene, music cues were written in weird time signatures, like 7/8 or

12/8. A time signature designates the number of beats to a measure and the note value for one beat. Rock & roll is usually written in 4/4, with a quarter note getting one beat with four beats to the measure. Cues usually have no key signature. Everything is kept atonal, which means that there is no real tonal center. This technique gives the composer the freedom to write music to fit the scene without being bound by the restrictions of harmony. The chords are sometimes written in clusters of dissonant notes as well as the normal harmonic chords used in popular music today.

In addition to my work on *S.W.A.T.*, I was on call to back up various artists on the *Midnight Special Show* on NBC. The show was taped in front of a live audience, but anytime there was a mistake the producers stopped the tape and did it over. Live TV audiences in L.A. are the best and most experienced on the planet. They yell and scream right on cue and patiently wait for retakes without complaining—unbelievable.

On one show featuring artists of the fifties, I played backup guitar for Frankie Avalon, Bobby Vinton, Fabian, the Fleetwoods, and other acts. It was a real fun time for me because I had learned all of their songs when I was growing up. All of the artists were very cool and easy to work with. In fact, after we played "Venus," Frankie Avalon came over and thanked me for playing the guitar part exactly like the record, even though it wasn't really written on the music chart.

I was also called to do a few *In Concert* live shows for ABC. One particular show stands out in my mind. The show featured the Temptations, and everything that could go wrong on that show did. As a studio musician, you learn patience and how to stay focused on the job at hand, which is pretty much what I did that day. I was pleasantly surprised a few weeks later when I received a big thank-you letter signed by all the of the Temptations, saying, "In the face of adverse conditions, you were a foundation of solid rock for us, and we'll never forget it! Please allow us to humbly say, Thank You!" That was the only time in my entire career when anyone bothered to send me a thank-you letter.

When I was working on *Midnight Special*, a friend of mine, Ernie Watts, who was on staff as a saxophone player in the band on the

Tonight Show starring Johnny Carson, invited me to lunch at the NBC commissary. He introduced me to trumpet player and band-leader Doc Severinsen, who came over to the table. After lunch, while I was still on break from *Midnight Special*, Ernie made sure I had a front-row seat for the taping of Carson's show.

I really enjoyed the show, and I realized I'd had a few misconceptions about how it was done. When I saw the show on my TV screen, I thought Johnny was performing in this huge theater with hundreds of people cheering and clapping. But even when the auditorium was packed I was surprised that there was only room for an audience of about one hundred people. I was also surprised to see Johnny read most of his monologue from cue cards. On my TV set at home, Johnny always looked like he was just standing up in front of an audience telling jokes. Well, that was Hollywood—the masters of illusion. After I saw the live show, I discovered that when I looked at Carson's eyes during his opening monologue I could see them move subtly as he read the cue cards.

L.A. was the land of celebrities. If you counted the music business, TV, and movies, L.A. probably had more stars per square mile than any other city in the world. You never knew which star you might see on the street or in a restaurant. One night I was working with Mike Theodore, and I looked up to see Paul McCartney walk through the door arm in arm with vocalist Peggy Lee. They both smiled and said hello and then went into one of the studios. I read in *Billboard* that they were recording a project together. I was surprised and a little jealous at how young Paul still looked back then in the seventies.

One night after work, Mike Theodore and I went to the L.A. Playboy Club. We'd never been there before, and we wanted to hear Kia Winding, the jazz trombonist who was performing there that night. After the show, we introduced ourselves to Kia. I also noticed that comedian Redd Foxx was seated at a table in the audience.

I walked over to him and introduced myself. I told him how much I had enjoyed his work over the years, and Redd told me he was a friend of Clarence Avant's. He invited Mike and me over to his table and turned out to be one of the most genuinely funny guys I had ever met. He had both of us in stitches the entire night, and my stomach was actually sore from laughing so hard. I had seen the *Redd Foxx Show* so much on television that I felt like I'd known him all my life.

Later a man named Mickey Cohen and his entourage came over to the table. I knew that Mickey was a gangster, but it wasn't until I later read a book about his life that I found out all the gory details. He was accompanied by a blonde bombshell and a sinister-looking bodyguard, who both looked like they had come out of central casting. When I needed cigarettes, Mickey just snapped his fingers and the waitress came right over and went and got me a pack.

Mike didn't know who Mickey was, and since we were all drinking and having a good time he invited Mickey to our next recording session. This was probably not the wisest thing to do. I kept trying to kick Mike under the table to get his attention so he would stop. I had exaggerated visions of Mickey or his bodyguard taking offense at our music and shooting up the control room, which had actually happened once in a studio in Detroit. I felt relieved when Mickey graciously declined.

As the night progressed, I found out that there was going to be a Foxx Roast for Redd at the Century Plaza. He invited us, so Mike and I took our wives. What a wild night it turned out to be! All the comedians in L.A. were there: Steve Allen, Milton Berle, Flip Wilson, Richard Pryor, and many others. For just one night, we felt like part of the Hollywood in crowd.

My story on the West Coast would not be complete without mention of the city and playground of the stars, Las Vegas. Las Vegas was a short flight from the Burbank airport, so Kathy and I went there a few times with Pat and Mike to see the sights, including one weekend when Wilson Pickett was appearing in one of the lounges.

When you sit at the gambling tables, pretty young cocktail waitresses in short skirts and low-cut tank tops keep you supplied with free drinks, so it doesn't take too long in the excitement of the moment to get a little hammered. I should have noticed that I was getting a little drunk at the blackjack table when the dealer caught me holding on twenty-three. The dealer made a big deal about it, so I decided to take a break from cards, or I think the dealer decided for me. I left the table, and we all went out to the lounge to find a good seat to see my old buddy Wilson's act. As Mike, Pat, and Kathy sat down, I excused myself to go to the bathroom. I never got back.

Things were a little fuzzy for me that night in Vegas, but I remember going backstage to visit Pickett, who was very glad to see me. The next thing I knew the curtain opened and I was in the show jamming with Wilson and his band.

The guitar player in the band didn't have anything to play because I was using his guitar, so he operated the special effects. He must have been bored because I was in the middle of a solo when he began clicking echoes and fuzz tones on and off at the most inappropriate times. I never knew what to expect from one song or solo to the next, but I was still having fun.

Unfortunately, I had neglected to tell Kathy, Mike, and Pat where I was going, so they had been taking turns looking for me out in the lobby. Poor Mike had even looked in the bathroom under the stalls to see if I had passed out in there. They finally gave up, sat down to enjoy the show, and were surprised to see me onstage.

Despite the excitement of the L.A. scene, I eventually got tired and burned out. I was playing too many recording sessions, TV shows, and even jingles. I played commercials for Goodyear Tire and did a Helena Rubenstein commercial featuring Johnny Mathis. Most of the time, I just read the music. There wasn't any room in the music for me to improvise or kick out the jams like I used to do in Detroit. To me, that was what made the Motown Sound so great.

In L.A., Clarence Avant was having problems with Sussex Records. I knew it was only a matter of time before they closed, so I negotiated another label deal for Mike Theodore and myself with Armen Boladian, the president of Westbound Records in Detroit. When I told Clarence that we wanted to move on, he graciously let us out of our Sussex contracts. I don't think the money was there to keep us on salary anyway. We began working for Westbound Records, and Armen suggested we go back to Detroit to record some music tracks. After a few sessions, I discovered that a new generation of funky players had taken center stage in Detroit. Besides that, I was homesick, so I moved back to continue to work for Westbound in 1976.

I had accomplished or tried everything I intended to do in L.A., and I couldn't wait to get back to the more open spaces of Michigan. There, within half an hour's drive, I could reach the serenity of the woods. I don't do well in crowded places, and I guess Detroit and Michigan are just in my blood. I'll probably live here until I die.

Back Home

I was really excited to be back in the Motor City. I still had my cottage on Stag Island in Canada, and all of my relatives were still in Detroit. We bought a two-story house on two acres of land, which included an acre of woods, in West Bloomfield. The house was spectacular and looked like a miniature version of the old southern plantation house from *Gone With The Wind.* Our house had two big, white columns in the front, overlooking a lush green lawn, and there was a long circular driveway leading up to the front door. Man, I really loved that house. I used to sit in my kitchen in the morning writing songs while watching pheasants, chipmunks, and woodchucks feeding in my backyard. That was my dream house: being so close to the woods, it made me feel peaceful, spiritual, and extremely creative.

Mike and I began our new production duties for Westbound in Detroit by recording most of the artists currently signed to the label, including me. In our enthusiasm to be good company employees and to help Armen record all his acts, we overlooked one basic thing: all of his existing acts were over thirty-five while the market was made up of kids buying records made by other kids. We should have realized this and signed younger talent, but these acts were into Armen for big money and he was trying to recoup some of his investment dollars.

In an effort to find some younger acts, we decided to take a stab at the disco dance market, which was just taking off. As part of my research, I went out and purchased the latest disco hits and analyzed their sound to see what made them tick. Once we had an idea of what made up the disco sound, we looked around for a group that would help us enter the market. We found it in the two girls and three guys who made up the group C. J. and Company.

The members of C. J. and Company were all in their early twenties, just the right age for the market in the late seventies. We selected a song called "Devil's Gun" by writers Green, Roker, and Shury in London, England. After recording it, we hired Tom Molton, disco mixer extraordinaire, to mix the song at Sigma Studios in Philadelphia. The group, the song, and the mixer proved to be a winning combination. "Devil's Gun" went on to become a disco classic and a number-one R&B record as well.

I was really excited about the record and thought it had "hit" written all over it. Armen, the president of Westbound, and the promotion staff at Atlantic Records didn't share my enthusiasm. They waited too long to cross the record over to the pop charts, so it never went the entire distance. "Devil's Gun" didn't sell a million copies, and it never received a gold record. I knew deep down in my heart that it was a hit record, but success in the music business can be as elusive as a butterfly floating on the wind in the middle of a hot summer day.

"Devil's Gun" was the last chance Westbound Records had with Atlantic to come through with a hit. Shortly afterward, in 1978, without much notice or fanfare, Atlantic Records quietly cut Westbound loose and Armen cut Mike and me loose. Goodbye, so long, no more salary—the end.

For the first time since I got out of the army, I was out of work and up the proverbial creek without a paddle. It was pretty scary after I got over the anger and shock of losing my job so abruptly. I had five kids at home to support, a house payment, two car payments, and cottage taxes to pay.

At first, Mike and I found a few investors and got three record deals going, but once the albums were completed the record companies began to have second thoughts and canceled the deals one by one. In one month, we lost deals with CBS, MCA, and TK Records, all because the record business was taking the plunge into its first recession. We should have seen the signs coming, but the record business was a still a young growth industry and everyone thought the money and good times would never end.

While trying to regroup, I played guitar on weekends with an oldies band and placed an ad in the paper for guitar students. I got a lot of response and ended up teaching in a house in Highland Park, which Mike had inherited from his family.

I decided to get a second mortgage from the bank to tide me over while I contemplated my next strategy. Finally, after much thought and serious soul searching, I decided to move one more time. Since Westbound Records had lost their deal with Atlantic and Motown had long since moved to L.A., Detroit had no more record companies left. If I was going to stay in the record business, I had to go to the source, and New York City had more record companies than anywhere else. That's where I decided to go.

"I'd rather lose everything I have trying to make it," I said to Mike Theodore one day, "than stay here and do nothing."

Little did I know how these words would come back to haunt me later.

Moving to the Big Apple

In September of 1979, I went to New York City and stayed at the famous Mayflower Hotel on Central Park West. The Mayflower was an exclusive hotel, catering to guests from all over the world. It was in a huge building, complete with a doorman and all the other comforts discriminating hotel guests have learned to expect.

The Mayflower had the most delicious and exquisite seafood salad I've ever tasted. I used to order the salad for dinner with fresh, warm bread, and wash it all down with a few ice cold gin martinis. Then I would sit back and watch the world go by on Central Park West and in Central Park across the street. The window of the restaurant was a marvelous place to people watch. I tried to imagine where all the people were going in such a big hurry and what they did for a living.

There were two things about the people on the street in midtown Manhattan that I never got used to: the number of homeless people panhandling and sleeping in doorways and the number of troubled souls wandering around all day talking to no one in particular.

One hot, muggy, summer afternoon as I was walking in midtown, I counted at least five different people walking next to me, muttering and talking. It was as if they were trying to exorcise their inner demons by talking and shouting into the sea of humanity passing them by. I assumed that most of them were harmless, but I wondered where they all lived and slept. How did they survive? In the past, I'd read stories about the homeless people in New York, but I never found the answers.

Of course, there was also excitement, and the excitement continued all night long, except for that special hour just before sunrise when everything became quiet and everyone disappeared, as if obeying some inaudible command to go home. At that hour, all things seemed strangely silent and at peace—peace that lasted only until the early risers appeared to greet the new day and to begin the sequence of living all over again.

While staying at the Mayflower, I intended to reconnoiter the housing situation in the New York area and select the place where my family and I would live. Obviously, in my financial condition I couldn't even consider buying a house. I knew I'd have to rent. I finally selected a small town in New Jersey called Glen Ridge.

Glen Ridge was a quaint little town straddling a two-mile stretch of Glen Ridge Boulevard. It had a post office and one high school. Most of the homes on the main street in Glen Ridge were huge, two-story, ivy-covered castles with deep, rich histories. I rented a brick house on a quiet neighborhood street leading to the Glen Ridge Country Club. On a clear day, from the dining room of the club I could see the impressive Manhattan skyline.

Once I got my family settled in, our first plan of attack was to try and secure record deals on projects we had already completed. Little did I know that conditions were so bad in the record business that companies like Warner Brothers had issued memos to all departments putting a six-month hold on signing new artists.

This was not a good time for the record industry and certainly not a good time for us to be trying to place new product. As Mike and I tried to move our business forward, the record industry got even worse. In the CBS building known as "The Black Rock," CBS let go of three hundred employees in a single day. Atlantic Records fired eleven people the same week, gutting an entire department. Afterward insiders at Atlantic referred to that day as Black Thursday.

Independent labels like Stax in Memphis and TK Records in Miami went under for good. Philadelphia International, under record producers Gamble and Huff, also ceased to exist. Many of my friends in the business lost their jobs or were transferred to places like Australia or England. Mike and I had absolutely no luck placing anything. As far as our production company was concerned, we were dead in the water.

Mike suggested that we try to buy an interest in a recording studio, which would give us jobs and a place to record. We looked at a few studios in the area and decided to invest in a small one in Montclair, New Jersey. At the last minute, the owner changed his mind and the deal went sour.

Finally, Mike and bassist Bob Babbitt bought an interest in Planet Sound in New York City. I backed out at the last minute because I didn't want to spend the rest of my career engineering recording sessions for other producers. Mike enjoyed being an engineer, but I still considered myself a guitar player and a producer. I just couldn't sit quietly and operate the control board if one of my customers was recording an inferior product. I knew I'd have to say something, which would be the end of my engineering career.

I did play on a few recording sessions at Media Sound in midtown Manhattan for my friend Charles Kipps, who was Van McCoy's ("The Hustle") partner. In the seventies, Charles and Van produced artists such as Aretha Franklin and David Ruffin.

I also wrote songs in my basement demo studio with a singer named Fonzie Thorton, a background studio singer in New York. Fonzie also sang for R&B star Luther Vandross.

I had few opportunities to record in major studios such as Sigma Studios, Media, and the Record Plant. One time in the studio I saw Ashford & Simpson, who were working on a project. I had played on all the songs they produced at Motown, so I walked over to say hello. I told them I was now living in New York and available for sessions. Of course, they never called.

When my telephone stopped ringing, it was as if I had leprosy or halitosis. Some days it felt like I had the kiss of death.

I did one session in New York for my old Motown buddy Hank Cosby, Stevie Wonder's producer. We cut some nice tunes, but I don't know what happened to them. During the session, I recalled that it was Hank, along with James Jamerson, who had hired me to work at the Motown Producer's Workshop at Golden World Studios in the first place, which led to all the sessions I played at Motown. It was like coming full circle.

In the early eighties, New York was a town filled with fancy, expensive restaurants and exclusive dance clubs. One of the most famous and exclusive dance clubs of them all was Studio 54, which received all the press and was known as a celebrity hangout. Rumor had it that if you were rich and famous enough at Studio 54 you could get away with anything, from sniffing cocaine on coffee tables in the back room to whatever else struck your fancy.

For the average citizen of New York, unless you could add to the ambiance and social mix, gaining entrance was almost impossible. Outside the club, on Fifty-fourth Street, you could always see a long line of hopefuls and wannabes anxiously waiting to get in.

The entrance to the club was roped off and viciously guarded by a huge doorman, who was meaner than a junkyard dog and twice as nasty. Of course, every time a big limousine pulled up and discharged a load of "swells," the change in the doorman was nothing short of miraculous. He'd suddenly turn into a charming maître d', fawning over the rich and famous. He knew which side his bread was buttered on. It was democracy and the golden rule, "He who has the gold rules," in action again.

"The Rock & Roll Kid," who was no longer rich and famous but was still experienced in deceiving the most discerning and pugnacious doormen, took evasive action. I told the doorman that the DJ was expecting me and gave him my name. I had no idea who was playing records that night, but with the success of "Devil's Gun" and my presence at many national *Billboard* disco conventions the DJ always let me in. I was ushered right into the DJ's booth, and then, after a short visit with my surprised host, the manager would escort me to the VIP section.

Another famous dance club in New York was Zenon's. I remember being ushered into the VIP section one night and finding Geraldo Rivera and Christopher Reeves sitting there at separate tables. The other people in the club were staring at us with curiosity. I'm sure they had no trouble recognizing Geraldo and Superman, but they were trying to figure out who I was. To me it only mattered that "The Rock & Roll Kid" himself always knew who he was.

The last time I saw my friend Del Shannon I was in New York

City at the Lone Star Cafe. That night I took Kathy, my oldest daughter Jordan, and her boyfriend to see Del play. Del looked fine singing onstage with a band of young kids backing him up. He sounded just like the same old Del playing his previous hits, which were mixed with selections from his successful new album, produced by rocker Tom Petty.

As I sat there and listened to Del, I was taken back in time. Most of the songs he played in the show were songs I had recorded with him. The kicker for me came in his finale, when he played "Move It On Over," a song he and I had written together. Del didn't even know I was in the audience, and I hadn't seen or spoken to him in almost twenty years.

When I went back to his dressing room to say hello, Del freaked out.

"Dennis?" He looked at me and shook his head back and forth a few times. "Man, how the hell are ya?"

"I'm fine, Del," I said. "How the hell are you?"

"What you been doin' all these years?" Del asked with genuine enthusiasm. "Where's Bob Babbitt?"

Bob had been a member of the Royaltones when we recorded with Del in New York. I told Del that he was living in New Jersey like me and doing sessions in New York.

We talked a little about old times, and then he suddenly looked over and noticed that someone had ripped up the jacket he'd left hanging in the tiny dressing room.

"What the hell happened to my jacket?" Del muttered as he lifted it off the hook and felt the torn pockets. "Some son of a bitch ripped it all up!"

"Welcome to New York City," I said, and shook my head in disgust. "I guess you just can't trust anyone anymore."

"I didn't even have anything worth stealing," Del complained.

"Well," I said, "I have to go back to Jersey. I'd better get moving before it gets too late. You still sound good Del. Take care of yourself."

I wondered how Del felt. He was at least my age, and he was touring the country working small clubs instead of concerts. He had been singing and playing the same old material the same way all these years. In the early years, the music scene was new and exciting, the money was fantastic, and everyone loved you. Now some of it had to be getting a little stale.

I could never spend the rest of my life out on the road playing the same songs day after day. I think Rick Nelson said it best in "Garden Party," a song he wrote about one of his appearances on an oldies show at Madison Square Garden in New York City. In the song, he said, "If memories were all I sang, I'd rather drive a truck."

If I had to play "Scorpio" all the time, it would drive me crazy. As a studio guitar player, I had been spoiled rotten—not only because I got to play with some of the greatest musicians in the world but because I got to play new songs every day. Recording music was like painting a picture. Every time you created a record in the studio you were creating a permanent work of art.

I was saddened and shocked when, in February of 1990, I heard of Del's tragic death from a self-inflicted gunshot wound at his home in California. Despite the time we had worked together, I felt I never really got to know him. He was a very private person. Being that way myself, I respected his space. We all have our inner demons chasing us, and I think in his case they caught up with him much too soon.

I also saw singer-songwriter Tommy Boyce again in New York when he was performing at a club on the upper east side. I hadn't seen him in twenty years, and until I mentioned the name of producer Harry Balk he didn't remember exactly who I was. Once he remembered me, he bought me a drink and we talked about old times. Then he went back to finish his show after telling me he was writing some new material with the guy who wrote "Tie a Yellow Ribbon," the gigantic hit for Tony Orlando and Dawn in the seventies. I felt a slight cringe when he said that because I had passed on "Tie A Yellow Ribbon" for a hit group I had produced called the Gallery. At the time, I'd felt the song was a little too square for the group.

I felt bad when I read later in the paper that Tommy Boyce had also shot himself. He had moved to Nashville. I wondered if he had relocated there to try to rejuvenate his songwriting career.

When my career got cold, I could imagine and identify with some of the pressures that both Del and Tommy must have been under. The music business is not a kind and friendly place to artists who lose their status and popularity. Rest in peace guys!

New York, New York

The last time I hung out with Wilson Pickett, we were at the Ritz in New York to hear Bobby Womack. Pickett had talked to Bobby beforehand, and he said we could sit in. After the show began, we headed toward the stage.

As we got close to the stage, a burly guard stopped both of us, thinking we were fans trying to crash the show. They wouldn't let me sit in because Ron Wood, the guitarist from the Rolling Stones, was up on stage playing. To top it all off, Bobby gave Pickett only three minutes to sing, an insult to an artist of Wilson's stature. I said the hell with it, and we went back to our table and sat down.

Pickett came over and suggested we go backstage and hang with the Kats after the show.

"No way," I said. "I didn't get a chance to play, and on top of that the stage guard treated me like a potential assassin. I think I'll call it a day and go on home."

The next day, I talked to Pickett on the telephone, and he told me how lucky I was that I hadn't stayed. After the show ended, he'd gone backstage and ended up getting into a fight with a Hell's Angel. The guy stabbed him in the head with a knife.

"I got blood all over my Mercedes because of that son of a bitch," Pickett yelled. "I had to hold my handkerchief to my head to stop the bleeding with one hand and drive all the way home to Jersey with the other! Some folks just ain't got no class."

If I was Pickett, I guess I'd be outraged too. But more than that, I'd be glad I was still alive. I wondered what Pickett might have done to provoke the attack. Maybe nothing. I didn't ask, but they don't call him "Wicked Pickett" for nothing. Of course, the Hell's Angels aren't exactly known for their restraint and peace-loving ways either.

There seemed to be a lot of work for musicians in both New York and L.A. New York had Broadway shows, *David Letterman, Saturday Night Live,* recording sessions, and jingles, all which paid musicians good money. But in my opinion L.A. had more opportunities. L.A. had more recording studios, film work, live TV shows, and jingles, which helped to eliminate some of the pressure and competition in the studio session business. There was usually something going on for musicians in L.A. But you had to be a proven commodity who knew the right people and had established a track record. Even joining the musician's union was tough. When I joined Local 47 in L.A., I had to go to the union office and sign in once a week for at least twelve weeks to prove I actually lived in L.A.

But, unlike New York and Detroit, L.A had very few clubs with live music. It was more of a tourist and restaurant town. Most club work never paid that much, but if you're a starving or new musician club work can come in handy.

If you calculated the number of musicians from all five boroughs of New York, New York State, Jersey, and Connecticut, there were a lot of players looking for work. I think that's what made the musicians in New York so competitive. I almost got into a fistfight once in a bar in New York because I was talking to the owner while another guitar player was sitting on the other side of her, trying to line up a one-night gig. I think he was upset because she liked my guitar playing and had one of my records on the jukebox.

No matter what I tried in New York, I couldn't get any work. I played a few jobs one night and did some recording sessions, but for the most part I came up dry. As I drowned my sorrows in martinis, it must have been very difficult for my family. It probably seemed like I was beginning to self-destruct. I tried everything I knew to find work, but the record business was stuck in a severe recession and I had lost the magic touch. I was out of luck.

When you're a studio hired gun in your prime and everything you touch turns to gold, you can do no wrong. You are very well paid for your work, but you never get really rich. That's reserved for the big artists and record executives. When you get past a certain age and people stop buying your records, you can only head for the showers. It can be a slow process, but one day you wake up and take stock of everything and it's all gone.

I often wondered how well my albums would have sold if I hadn't squandered so much of my creativity at Motown and other record companies. At one time in my career, I was on so many hit records that I couldn't remember them all. If I had known then what I know now, I might have taken a different approach. But I had a family to support and needed a dependable income, so I tried to cut down on all the risks as much as I could.

One day, while sitting in my kitchen in New Jersey taking stock of my life, my bank account, and my future, I made the decision to move back to Detroit. At least I had friends and family back there who would help, and Detroit wasn't as congested and competitive as New York. I was sorry to leave my good friends Charles Kipps and Mike Theodore, but I had to do whatever it took to keep going.

Being out of work and unable to support your family can feel like having a disabling disease. It can paralyze you with fear, erode your self-esteem, and chip away at your sense of self-worth. Your job and profession are who you are. What you do to earn your living is a thread that runs deep, a thread that stays connected to the very means of prolonging life itself. It helps you provide the three necessary items to sustain life—food, shelter, and the clothes on your back. Losing that thread is one of the most traumatic and stressful experiences anyone can have.

I still had enough money left in the bank to pay a moving company and rent a house back in Detroit, so I began looking for work in Michigan. One day I got lucky and found an ad in the paper for a sales job with a company selling directories to hotels. The company was located in Kent, Ohio, and had reached the point where it was ready to expand its business by hiring sales representatives to work the four surrounding states.

I drove to Ohio from New Jersey, interviewed with the company executives, and got the job. They agreed to pay me three hundred dollars per week plus bonuses to cold call on hotels and convince them to allow us to place our directory in a conspicuous place in the lobby. The directory was a large, wooden, colorful map of the area. Local merchants paid for ads on the board. When you pressed a button next to an ad, it made the location light up and showed you how to get to there from the hotel.

Once the hotel agreed to place the directory in its lobby, another sales representative would come in and sell advertising space to the local merchants. That was how the company made its money. Any job that would get my family and me back to the Detroit area was worth a shot, so I signed on.

My fall from grace was a long one. I had spent my entire life as a musician and writer in the record business and had reached the top of my profession. I was still a high-strung, talented musician who didn't have a college degree or anything else to fall back on. I had planned to be in music my entire life, so I wasn't prepared to do anything else.

Back in the Big "D"

Once I got the job, I drove back to Detroit and rented a house in Farmington Hills so my oldest son Dennis would be back with his friends. When we first moved to New Jersey, Dennis was so mad over leaving his friends that he didn't speak to me for three months. It was my mistake to move there, so I felt the least I could do was to help him get his life back to normal again.

It felt good to be back in Detroit, but I was just beginning to fight the first battle of the long war ahead of me to regain financial independence outside of the music business. The New York fiasco cost me my life savings of about seventy thousand dollars, which in the eighties was a lot of money. I felt like I was the only person in the world who had been let down by the American Dream. No one was more dedicated to music than I was. No one worked more hours than I did, and still, in the end, it didn't really matter. I still hit the skids.

I got my next job by answering an ad in the local paper for a guitarist to play in a Top 40 band. Nobody wanted to book me as a recording artist, but I had worked in a Top 40 band to pay the bills in the old days, so I gave it a try. I got the job after an audition with the band, which featured singer Debbie Owens. Debbie wanted to establish a recording career. Mike and I had recorded a country record on her some time ago, so I was surprised to see her again.

The band had a booking agent, who had twenty bands just like us. He told us what clothes to wear, what type of songs to play, and what type of sound system and lights we needed. He told us everything we needed to know but left out one important piece of information: he couldn't guarantee us steady work. Because most of the booking agents in Detroit negotiated agreements with different club owners, they really didn't represent the musicians. I found this odd, since two of the biggest agencies were owned by musicians.

The booking agents made sure all the bands dressed the same and sounded the same so that, if a club owner didn't like a band, the group could be immediately replaced with another. It was a great system for the club owner and the booking agent, but we were out of work for two or three weeks at a time.

If you live in Detroit, almost everyone you meet has spent some time working in an automobile factory. This town was built on cars and trucks, which is, after all, why it's called the Motor City. My mother worked for Packard Motors, and my stepfather worked the line at GM. In those days, all you needed was a strong back, a willingness to work, and the desire for a decent-paying job at one of the many auto plants that dotted the area.

One day I ran into my brother-in-law, Chuck Zajac, a manager at GM. Chuck told me that GM was going to be hiring and suggested that I apply for work there. I had to apply through the Michigan Employment Security Commission (MESC) because at the time competition for jobs on the assembly line was intense. I went down to the MESC and completed an application. Then I drove home and waited for the call.

Finally, I received a call from the MESC. I was told to come down to the office and take a battery of tests. The Big Three had assigned them to screen all potential job candidates—quite a change from the old days, when a person could get a job by walking in the door of a plant and completing an application.

There were so many job applicants that the MESC had to rent a hall to accommodate all of us for testing. I took four intelligence tests in the morning and a manual dexterity test in the afternoon. For the dexterity test, they gave me a big board and told me to place small screws and parts together. I had always done well on tests, plus I had fast guitar-playing fingers, so I blew through it at about ninety miles an hour. No one else, young or old, could match my speed that day. I was awesome.

The MESC told me I had passed all the tests and that I would be hearing from the plant to take a drug screen. If I passed that, I'd get hired. I waited and waited, and nothing happened. I called my brother-in-law, and he said he'd check into it. The next day he called me and said they'd already given everyone the drug screen. Someone at the plant had removed my application and replaced it with the application of one of their relatives, not knowing that I had a contact working there as well.

Chuck told me to come in Saturday for my drug screen. He had the power to authorize it. That was how I finally got hired at GM to work on the assembly line at my age. I had no idea what I was getting into. I had never been inside an automotive plant in my life, but I knew I needed the steady work and insurance coverage for my family. Kathy was also working, but she wasn't making enough to support our family. We had bill collectors driving us crazy.

I was scheduled to report to work at the GM plant in August of 1985. "The Rock & Roll Kid" would now take his place on the assembly line, like his parents and many Detroiters before him. I didn't have any idea what I was getting myself into, but I had no choice. I still had three kids left at home to support, so I plunged ahead.

Generous Motors

What the hell was happening? The hot summer night was stifling, humid, and sticky. Damn, it must have been 120 degrees inside! The noise all around me was deafening. All I could hear was the loud crashing of gigantic machines while an angry red mist swirled in the air and covered everything as far as I could see. By the end of each day, my clothes and even the pores of my skin were saturated with the foul, syrupy, red fluid.

My arms moved in and out like pistons. My body was like a robot. Turn around . . . bend over . . . pick up the torque converter . . . stand up . . . turn around . . . place it in a transmission moving down the line. I performed the same iron ballet three times a minute on autopilot. I did the same job 180 times an hour, 1,620 times a day, for nine to ten hours a day. I usually worked five or six days a week.

I was part of a huge machine made of one hundred other parts moving with precision clockwork in and out of final assembly line 3—moving parts that were in reality a hundred living and breathing souls working like angry bees buzzing around a hive—human bees that kept hovering, tending a moving mechanical line that seemed to go on forever.

The assembly line was a chain-link monster moving with a life of its own on huge gears and wheels. The heavy conveyer emerged from a dark pit in the floor like some prehistoric creature rising out of primordial slime. When it reached the end of its journey through the plant, the monster disappeared back down into the same dark pit.

Another huge, automated conveyer slowly moved in and out of the ceiling beams before it crossed over from the transmission case job and arched down to the floor in front of the line. At the front of the line, a "factory rat" named Bill lifted an empty transmission case dripping hot fluid off the conveyer. He was sweating profusely and grunting under the strain. Bill was wearing a red headband to keep the sweat from running into his eyes and clouding his vision. He was also wearing a white T-shirt with the sleeves cut out, dirty blue jeans, and steel-toed safety boots. He secured each transmission in place on a stand moving down the line.

Bill had to load transmissions on the line three times a minute to keep up with the line. He was wearing yellow disposable earplugs because the noise level was equal to that of a jet plane taking off. Most of the time he worked alone, isolated in his own mind, separated from the sounds around him by an eerie, stuffed silence. As he worked, he appeared to be dreaming of better times and happier places. He once told everyone on the line that he used to be a manager for a trucking company. Maybe he saw himself back behind that fancy desk in his office before the company went belly up in the early seventies, pulling the rug out from under him. Now, with only a year of college and no degree, he was working on line 3.

At the end of the line, John, another factory rat, swung around a pneumatic lift on a cable, hooked a fully built transmission like a fat bass on a fishing plug, and lifted it off the line. He swung it around and placed it on another automated conveyer, which took it to another department to be buttoned-up and shipped to a final automotive body assembly plant. In his mind, John was probably on one of those famous fishing trips he was always talking about. Judging by the faraway look in his eyes, he could have been on a clear green lake loaded with plump, feisty trout.

John had drunk a few too many beers at the three bars strategically located across the street from the plant and had a belly hanging over his belt. He told his coworkers that the beer helped to numb the pain he felt in his arms and lower back from doing the same repetitive work each day. John was wearing a sweat-stained Harley David-son T-shirt with faded blue jeans, while splashy red tattoos of motor-cycles and American flags danced on his arms in the dim, smoky light. As he worked, the huge silver chain connecting his belt to the keys and wallet in his back pocket jingled with every move. Greasy, worn, motorcycle boots completed his industrial wardrobe. Yet he was almost overdressed, considering the oily, grimy environment he worked in from day to day. Welcome to "Generous Motors" and final assembly line 3.

My mind was numb and my muscles ached as I worked and sweated in the intense heat of the plant. One day I heard music play-ing from somewhere down the line when another factory rat clicked on a boom box. The radio got louder and louder until the sound crashed through my brain like a thunderbolt and gave me the chills when I recognized "Cloud Nine" by the Temptations.

I listened to the funky groove of the music, and vivid memories exploded inside my head. The guitar solo in "Cloud Nine" rang loud and clear as it soared high above the loud noises and machinery on the line. As I recognized the sound of my wah-wah pedal guitar solo, I turned away sadly and shook my head in disgust. I just couldn't believe what had happened to me!

As I listened, Dennis Edwards belted out the lyrics, his voice crackling with energy as the rest of the group sang sweet background harmonies. As I worked, I felt the sweat running down my face and stinging my eyes. I wished I could be anywhere but here, humping this damn line for all I was worth. My hands ached, my back hurt like hell, and I felt like I was gonna die!

As the music continued to play, I stared mesmerized at my hands. Visions of them flying over the guitar fingerboard came rush-ing back. It seemed like only yesterday that these same hands were earning me a living in a very different way, at a house converted into a recording studio on Grand Boulevard in Detroit. In those days, I played guitar with one of the top recording bands in the world. We were a major part of the Motown Sound . . . hell, we were the Motown Sound!

At Motown, I worked with "Chunk of Funk," "Spider," "Soup-bone," "Bongo," and "Pistol" five days a week in a recording studio nicknamed the Snake Pit. Now I was a factory rat working on line 3 with "Crackhead," "Mad Dog," "Sarge," and "Superfly," watching my American Dream slowly die. For me, the dream had turned into an American nightmare.

I wondered where I'd gone wrong. When I was growing up, I'd believed in the American Dream—that if you worked like hell you'd be rewarded with a place at the table: a nice house, a car, a good standard of living, and security. After I damn near lost everything I had, I was working on the line trying to make a living and support my family, but I was paying a terrible price. After all, I was still a musician, and I should have been creating great music, not working like a robot.

My relationship with GM was always filled with both love and hate. On the one hand, I was grateful for the opportunity it gave me, but on the other hand I hated it for turning me into a piece of machinery. I always completed each job assigned to me, and did quality work, but I still felt like a robot. As a musician, my very existence used to depend on creating new ideas every day. Now the daily repetition of working the line was just the opposite.

I was suddenly and rudely jerked back to reality by a coworker who was yelling in my direction. I turned just in time to see a transmission about to go by without the torque converter.

"Shit," I muttered to myself, "I'd better load that transmission fast or I'll be in trouble big time." I ran over and loaded a torque converter into the transmission just before it reached the end of the line. I worked fast, trying to "stay out of the hole." Management set the line speed, and we were forced to stay on our toes to maintain the production quotas. If you stopped the line because you couldn't keep up, you'd soon regret it.

When I first got the job, I had nightmares for a week. Each night I woke up in a cold sweat. The nightmares were always the same: I was working on the line, trying to keep up, but no matter how fast or hard I worked I was still always in the hole. At the end of my nightmare, a big, nasty supervisor always ran over waving his arms, yelling at me, and threatening to fire me if I didn't keep up.

When you were new at any job on the line, the line speed created a stress all its own until you mastered the moves. Lucky for me, my coworkers usually pitched in to help until I got the hang of it. If I got behind, the person down the line from me usually signaled by waving his hand in the air.

"Stop the line!" He'd yell to everyone within hearing. He had to let everyone else know that I was putting him in the hole.

When that happened, the person who was closest to the stop button would shut off the line and a red light would flash, which usually brought a supervisor over to see what was really wrong.

There were some jobs on the line that were so hard on me I couldn't do them. I wasn't young enough, big enough, or strong enough to get it together and keep up. I always gave each job my best shot, but if it gave me trouble I stopped the line. After I had stopped the line a few times, the supervisor usually assigned me to another job. He knew I was doing my best and not goldbricking to get assigned an easier job.

The first job I had was one of the most difficult on the line. As a new hire, I always got the jobs the workers with higher seniority didn't want. New hires like me were also frequently used as floaters, which meant I had to learn a different job every day to replace whoever hadn't come to work. I learned all of the moves for each job in about two hours. In a day or two, I usually got "slick" on the job, which meant I had mastered the fastest way to do the job with the least amount of effort.

My first job at the plant was installing a thirty-five-pound torque converter in each transmission as it went down the line. The torque converter transferred the power, or torque, from the engine through the transmission to the wheels, which caused the car to move. There were very few volunteers for the torque converter job because it was so difficult. When I was first assigned the job, it was a two-man job.

My first day in the plant, a supervisor took me over to the line and introduced me to this tall, lanky African American guy wearing an old blue denim jacket with the sleeves cut out.

"Joe, here's your new helper," he said. "Teach him how to do the job."

The job was a real bitch. I was sweating almost immediately and had to wrap a rag around my head to keep the sweat from blinding me and stinging my eyes in the summer heat.

To accomplish the job, I had to turn around, bend over, and lift a converter out of a large square container called a skip, which had iron grill sides. Then I had to stand up, turn back, and seat the torque converter into a transmission moving down the line. The torque converter resembled a huge flying saucer filled with hot transmission fluid. There were three different splines inside, so I had to spin the torque converter—using the metal nipple on top—until all the splines lined up and it could be seated all the way down into the transmission. In order to keep up with the line, I had to place one torque converter in a transmission three times a minute.

The hardest part of the torque converter job was getting the splines to line up. Sometimes they wouldn't line up, and the torque converter wouldn't fit into the transmission no matter what I did. Then, I had to take it out and try another one. I usually had to wobble the torque converter back and forth with my hand, or spin it real fast to get it to seat. Everyone who did the torque converter job had a different technique for seating it, but nothing worked every time. In addition to being a difficult, sweaty job, the torque converter job chewed up my hands so bad that I had to stuff my work gloves with paper towels to cut down on the pain.

When factory rats got slick on a job and started goofing off—or working too fast—the managers did one of two things: they eliminated the job by dividing the work up between two adjacent jobs, thereby making those two jobs more difficult; or they made it a one-man job. It didn't matter to them how hard the job was; once they saw one man do it, however briefly, they were convinced it could be done that way forever. I was always the one who got left doing the job by himself.

After that first day, I went home every night with sore hands, an aching back, and smelling like transmission fluid. Each morning I woke up with numb, tingling hands and arms that felt like they were stuck with pins and needles. I didn't know if the job was doing any permanent damage to my hands, but as a guitar player I sure hoped it wasn't. Eventually, the pain got so bad that I went straight home after work every night and poured myself a few good belts of cheap scotch whiskey. Then I would fall into bed completely exhausted before drifting off into a deep, dreamless sleep. My wife Kathy couldn't understand why I didn't take a shower and wash off the transmission oil before climbing into bed. But when I tried to shower after work, the hot water would jerk me wide awake and I'd be up the rest of the night with nothing to do but stare at the four walls.

Finally, before my ninety days of probation time were up, a transmission repairman on the line found out that I was a guitarist. He went to the supervisor and convinced him to assign me to another job so my hands wouldn't be ruined for life. The supervisor agreed and took me off the torque converter job.

One day a new hire volunteered to replace me. He told the supervisor that the job looked like a piece of cake. He was a big, strapping blond kid. I figured he could handle it. Two weeks later I saw him walking by the line with both of his hands covered with bandages.

"Hey, kid," I said. "What happened with that torque job?"

He looked over my way, his cockiness completely gone.

"Man, that job almost wrecked my hands for life. I had to report to medical, and they sent me to the doctor. You want your old job back?"

"No way, man," I shouted. I laughed to myself and went back to my new job on the line.

While working on the line, I decided to record a new album using the songs I had written in New Jersey plus some new songs I'd completed since moving back to Michigan. A friend of mine, Tom Hayden, in L.A. had started an independent record label called TSR Records. He had expressed an interest in releasing my new songs.

George Katsakis, another old friend from the Royaltones days, agreed to assist me in the project and help raise the money to pay for it. The name of the album was *Motor City Magic*. I played acoustic guitar on most of the songs, and George played sax. I also hired two old Motown buddies, Earl Van Dyke on piano and Uriel Jones on drums. *Motor City Magic* was probably the last album Earl played on before he passed away.

To begin the project, I first spent some time writing the musical arrangements. After I finished the arrangements, I went into the studio and recorded every day, including weekends, before going to work on the line. When the album was released, it created quite a sensation among my fellow workers, especially when we heard it played on Detroit jazz radio station, WJZZ as we were humping the line. They couldn't understand why I wasn't out on the road playing. Unless you had a hit album or financial backing from the record company, it made little sense to go on the road. For a young person without family responsibilities it might work, but for a married man supporting a family—no way! I stuck it out and kept working on the line.

In the fall of 1988, my wife Kathy looked at me and told me I was no longer meeting her needs, which was probably true. Of course, she was no longer meeting my needs either. Still, I was so totally immersed in a life and death struggle to get off the assembly line— while continuing to support my family—that I didn't have much time for anything else.

That was the beginning and the end of our discussion and the end of our marriage as far as I was concerned. I knew we had grown far apart. Once she fired the first volley, I felt there was no turning back.

That night I moved into one of the boys' rooms. I wasn't sure if it was due to all the stress I was under or not, but the die had been cast and I was tired of fighting. I was worn out, and I decided to move on.

After we were divorced, we shared custody of our two sons, James and Andy. At first, they lived with Kathy, but before long they came to live with me and I began life again as a single parent. After my first divorce, I raised three kids on my own, so I knew I could raise my second two as well.

After working there a year and a half, I found out that they were looking for instructors in the plant. I gave them my resume and asked to be considered for the job. I listed on my resume that I had been a guitar teacher at Fava's Music in Oak Park. The plant joint leadership called me in for an interview. They asked me to memorize a long paragraph from a picture hanging on the wall and to teach it to them. They gave me about five minutes. I read the material, memorized it, and taught it to them. I must have passed the test, because I was soon notified that I had been selected to be an in-plant trainer and course developer.

At the Training Center, I attended eight weeks of classes in training needs analysis and evaluation, instructional design, course development, and delivery. I graduated and was certified as a GM trainer. I was now part of the training and course development team. We developed a forty-hour course on the theory of operations in which students learned to disassemble and assemble a transmission. I taught the class every week and remained on the team for the next two years.

Following a union election in 1989 at which the people who supported the training program had not been reelected, I found myself back on the line. I now had new skills and nowhere to apply them.

At this point, I'd already had two years of college. I decided to go back to Wayne State University in Detroit and get my bachelor's degree.

I enrolled in their College of Lifelong Learning for working adults. I discovered that I could take twelve credit hours a semester, which I did by taping one class a week on TV, taking one class a week at school, and taking one class over the weekend.

I also decided to look for another job. I would go to job interviews in a business suit, come to work at the plant, and change clothes in my car in the parking lot. Some days I felt like Clark Kent turning into Superman in a telephone booth.

After looking for about eight months, my job-hunting efforts paid off. In 1989, I interviewed for a job at a company called Detroit Art Services (DAS) and was hired as a course developer and technical writer. The company hired me because it had just received a request to develop a huge training program for the United Auto Workers (UAW) at Ford, and because of my experience developing courses and teaching at GM I was a natural.

As one of the conditions for employment, DAS insisted that I complete my college degree. I was so excited about the opportunity to get off the line and into an office, where I'd have my own cube, desk, and computer, that I was more than happy to agree. I was carrying a 3.6 average in school at the time, and I really enjoyed learning new things.

At DAS, I created and developed a training program on automotive technology for UAW-Ford. The program was a huge success and is still being taught in automotive plants all over the country. I was also the project manager for the program.

One day, Ken Cerny, vice president and instructional designer at DAS, happened to mention that Wayne State University now had a graduate program in instructional technology. I decided to go.

When I completed the big UAW-Ford project at DAS, which spanned almost three years from creation to implementation, I found that there was not enough work left to keep me busy all day, so I decided to leave. It had been an enjoyable three years, and I had learned many things there.

After trying a few other jobs and receiving my master's degree in instructional technology, I got a good job as the training manager for ISI Robotics. At ISI, I managed twelve trainers and technical writers and a six-thousand-square-foot training center.

My next career move brought me to MSX International and an assignment at a stamping plant for the Ford Motor Company. On this job, I managed the plant training system, supervised nine trainers, and attended Plant Operating Committee meetings regularly. After about a year and a half, I was offered a staff assignment in Dearborn supporting Ford's lean manufacturing efforts as a lean manufacturing instructor and a plant performance consultant.

In 1989, in the middle of all these new challenges in my life, I found the time to go into the studio and record my tenth album and first CD, entitled *Under the Moonlight,* which was released in 1990. My partners in this venture were Eric and Marilyn Morgeson, who owned Studio A in Dearborn Heights. This album was more widely received than *Motor City Magic* and went up to number four on the national Radio and Records New Adult Contemporary Chart. I signed a contract with the Orpheus record label, which was distributed by EMI. Shortly afterward, Orpheus lost its deal with EMI (now why does that sound familiar?), and my comeback shot was smashed to the ground once more. You'd think by now I'd wise up, but once a musician always a musician.

Epilogue

I was driving my red Probe down Beech Road on the outskirts of Detroit on the way to Studio A to arrange and produce my first record date in five years. Even though my last project had hit the skids, I was ready to try again. This was to be my eleventh album.

My son James was sitting next to me. He radiated the excitement of youth as he fired off a never-ending barrage of questions.

"Who's all going to be at the studio Dad?" It was question number twenty-two, but who was counting?

"A cooking rhythm section of musicians I handpicked myself," I said, keeping my eyes on the road.

"You mean there's going to be an entire band in the studio?"

"You got it."

I was so used to working in the recording studio that I sometimes forgot how new and exciting it was for James, who was coproducing the CD with me. James had never seen a live band in the studio in his entire life.

As we walked into the foyer, the first two people I saw were Marilyn and Eric Morgeson. They had been two of my biggest supporters and friends over the years, and they were my partners in this new CD project. Eric was the coproducer. He used to play keyboards in the Detroit Guitar Band and played on my album *Going For Myself.* He and his wife Marilyn also owned the recording studio. Studio A had been custom designed by the same man who designed Criteria Studios in Miami, where the Bee Gees and many other artists, including Stephen Stills, recorded many of their hits.

I was a little apprehensive as I walked into the control room. I'd written eleven songs, including a few with my son James. I knew Eric and Marilyn liked them, but I wasn't quite sure how my arrangements would turn out or how the musicians would perform. Detroit still has some of the finest players in the country, but I knew they didn't get the chance to do many complete rhythm sessions with a band anymore.

In the nineties, most recording sessions used new technologies: drum machines, synthesizers, and overdub musicians playing one at a time. I'd done my last album, *Under the Moonlight* that way. But this time I wanted to capture the creativity of the musicians bouncing ideas off each other and playing at the same time. I wanted to hear the interplay between musicians in the studio that I'd gotten used to at Motown and the synergy that resulted when the whole was greater than the sum of the individual parts. I felt that with my experience and direction, combined with a little patience, the six musicians I'd selected would be up to the challenge. I was sure they'd reward me with the kind of band tracks I wanted.

When I was writing the arrangements, I decided to use two percussionists, a drummer, a keyboard player, and a bass player to establish the foundation for the music tracks. I'd wanted to use two percussionists—a conga player and a tambourine player—because Motown always had. I missed that sound, and I wanted to try it again with a new generation of Detroit musicians.

One of the percussionists was Lorenzo Brown, affectionately known as "Bag-A-Tricks" or "Spoons." Spoons put on quite a show in clubs when he came out from behind his congas and went into the audience playing two ordinary tablespoons—tablespoons that sounded anything but ordinary in his hands.

On bass, I used Jimmy Ali, a great player, who also played on my *Under the Moonlight* CD. Jimmy had a great feel and really moved around on a six-string bass.

Once the session got under way, I did a double take when I saw

Jimmy sitting on a stool in the studio wearing the same kind of beret my Motown buddy, the late James Jamerson, used to wear. From where I was sitting in the control room, the resemblance was remarkable.

The other bass player on the CD was Al Turner. Al was another great player who worked with guitarist Earl Klugh.

The other percussionist on the session was Dennis Sheridan. I hadn't used him before, but he showed up on the session with all kinds of exotic percussion instruments and a positive attitude. I knew he was going to work out fine.

The drummer I picked for the session was Danny Cox. I'd first heard Danny together with Jimmy Ali, in Alexander Zonjic's band at Arriva's Restaurant in Warren. Alex, the bandleader, is a flamboyant flute player. He has a CD out on Warner Brothers and records with piano player Bob James. He is now a successful DJ on Smooth Jazz, V98.7.

When I heard Danny play that night, I knew he was the drummer I wanted to use on my CD. And as the session in the studio continued I knew I'd made the right choice. Danny added that extra creativity I was looking for to nail down the groove and drive the rest of the band.

As featured soloists, I used Earl Klugh on classical guitar, David McMurray on soprano sax, and Dwight Adams on trumpet. I also used Jerald Daemyon on electric violin and Ray Manzerolle on alto and tenor sax. These guys all did a fantastic job, especially jazz great Earl Klugh, who really impressed me with his ability and feel. I was also delighted with the new dimension Daemyon added to one song with his electric violin. On vocals and lyrics, I used Parks Stewart and two girls from the gospel group Witness. Not only did Parks add some great vocal tracks to the songs, but he wrote some great lyrics as well.

By the end of the first session, I knew I'd made the right choices. We recorded the first three songs just as I'd envisioned them. Later I added keyboardist and synthesizer player Louie Resto, who also worked on my previous albums. I also added Ollie Harris on drums, Wayne Gerard on rhythm guitar, and Aaron Lindsey on keyboards. I was now back in the saddle again in Detroit, working with both old and new friends and doing one of the things I love to do the best—creating great music!

FARMINGTON, 1999

One day, in 1999, I received a call from my friend Barry James. Barry is from York, England, and he used to make his home in the Detroit area. I originally met him at a bar and restaurant in Troy called Mr. B's, which is owned by Scott Forbes, a friend of mine and a country singer and writer. Barry called to tell me that some of his friends from England were in town and wanted to meet me. Barry had been telling them about the soul records I had played on in the early sixties and seventies. They were big fans of this music. I agreed to meet them, and that night I was introduced to a music phenomenon called Northern Soul. The term *Northern Soul* was coined in the sixties by Dave Godin, a respected soul music aficionado in England. In one of his magazine articles, David referred to the soul music being played in the clubs in northern England as Northern Soul, and the name stuck.

That day was the beginning of a few enjoyable evenings at Mr. B's with Northern Soul music fans from England, Detroit, and Toronto. The people I have met so far have been mainly record promoters, collectors, and DJs who were involved in the Northern Soul music scene in England in the seventies. Their knowledge and passion for this type of music is simply amazing. They seem to know about the many records I've played on, including some very obscure recordings that were done for small record labels in Detroit, such as Dearborn and Impact. These records didn't get much airplay in the states, so I didn't think anyone would notice them, but apparently I was mistaken. Some of their favorites were "Lucky Day" by the Theo-Coff Invasion, "Believe It Or Not" by Nabay, "Mind Intruder" and "Stop Don't Worry About It" by Lonette, "Sally Go Round The Roses" by Inner Circle, and "I Can Get Along" by the Strides.

FARMINGTON, 2001

I answered the telephone and was surprised to hear Allan Slutsky on the other end. Allan had written a book years ago about Motown bassist James Jamerson called *Standing in the Shadows of Motown: The Life and Music of Legendary Bassist James Jamerson.* I'd given Allan some Jamerson stories, and after the book was released he had called to tell me he was trying to put together a tour of the Funk Brothers. He'd asked me if I would be interested. I'd told Allan I had a good day job, and a solo career, and wouldn't be interested in leaving that to go on the road.

Since then, I'd heard they were making a documentary based on the book, but I assumed I wasn't going to be in it. This time Allan was calling to let me know that they were filming a live concert at the Royal Oak Theater with Ben Harper, Chaka Khan, Joan Osborne, Gerald Levert, and other recording artists.

"We're recording 'Cloud Nine,'" he said. "We want you to play for us and do your wah-wah thing."

This time I was happy to agree.

That Sunday I put my guitar and special effects gear in the trunk of my car and drove to the theater in downtown Royal Oak. By the time I got there, everyone was set up onstage for the rehearsal. I took a seat next to two of the Funk Brothers' guitarists, Joe Messina and Eddie Willis. I hadn't seen either one of them since the seventies.

It felt good to see my old friends again. I looked over and saw that the other surviving Funk Brothers were there too: Jack Ashford on tambourine, Johnny Griffith and Joe Hunter on piano, Pistol Allen and Uriel Jones on drums, and my old friend Bob Babbitt on bass. Missing were Earl Van Dyke on keyboards, James Jamerson on bass, Bongo Eddie on congas, and Robert White on guitar. They had all passed away. Also missing was Jack Brokenshaw, the vibe player who was on most of the sessions at Hitsville with us. I'd seen Jack at a jazz concert in the area a few years before, and he was still playing some great solos. I don't know why he wasn't here. I also didn't see any of the Motown arrangers, like Dave Van De Pitte and Paul Riser, either.

Allan walked over and handed me a guitar chart with "Cloud Nine" printed at the top of the page.

"Here is the part I want you to play," he said.

I looked at the guitar chart, and Allan counted off the tempo. I began to play the written part. I hadn't played "Cloud Nine" since 1968. I was working my way through the notes as the rest of the band played their charts. When we were about halfway through the song, Allan stopped the band. He walked over to me.

"Hey, Dennis," he said. "Can I see your guitar?"

"Sure," I said, and handed it over to him, wondering what he had in mind.

"This is how I want you to play your part," he said as he played.

It was the first time in my life that anyone had tried to show me how they wanted me to play a part that I had created. I was simply amazed! I could imagine what Jamerson would have done in this situation. Of course, I didn't say anything. I just played. During the rehearsal, I demonstrated to Allan how I used the wah-wah pedal to play the part. After the rehearsal, I said goodbye to the Funks, packed up my guitar, and drove back home to get ready for work the next day.

I waited during the following week and heard nothing from Allan. I figured maybe he was going to play my part himself because he had played some of Robert White's guitar parts during the film. I was surprised when Allan called me late Thursday night to do the session on Friday.

"Hey, man," he said. "We're ready for you. We're going to record tomorrow. Can you make it?"

By then it was too late. I had two important meetings scheduled for the next day that I couldn't miss. Allan decided they'd have to do it without me.

Even though I missed the concert, Allan called me again the following week and asked if I would come to Hitsville and do an interview for the film.

The last time I'd been in Motown Studio A was when I took the people from the Motown Museum and the Henry Ford Museum there. In the *Standing in the Shadows of Motown* documentary, Jack Ashford comments that you could still feel the creative vibes in the Snake Pit from everyone who'd worked so hard to make those hit records. On my last trip, when the people from the museum opened the door to the studio and we entered and walked down the steps, I'd felt those same vibes. I'd shown them where each musician sat and told them the kind of instrument they'd played. It was an eerie feeling, and it brought back memories of those who were no longer with us. Standing in the studio again, I could visualize Jamerson sitting on his stool, holding his bass, and chuckling, with a cigarette dangling from his lips. I could hear Bongo Eddie cracking his crazy Bullwinkle jokes from behind the girlie magazine on his music stand. I could see Robert sitting by the wall under the control room window, looking seriously at his music as he made sure he understood his part. I could feel Earl across the room practicing a few heavy dynamic chords on the piano.

I'd had a nice visit to the museum that day. I'd also donated to the museum a wah-wah pedal and the echoplex unit I'd used on "Ball of Confusion" and "Smiling Faces" and other songs as well.

This time when I entered the studio, I met Allan and the director, Paul Justin. I went in and sat down where I used to sit. I picked up the Gibson Firebird guitar from the stand and played it through my wah-wah pedal to warm up. Paul asked me a few questions, and we started the interview. I played guitar licks through the wah wah pedal and talked for about thirty minutes.

I think Allan accomplished a remarkable task by getting that movie funded and completed. It is a great movie, and all of the Funks were very excited and happy to get the recognition they finally deserved. Receiving two Grammy awards for the soundtrack was the icing on the cake.

The sad part of the story is that after the film was completed two of the Funk Brothers passed away. Pistol Allen died of lung cancer before the film was released, and Johnny Griffith died of a heart attack in his hotel room on the day of both the Detroit screening and a live concert at the Roostertail. That morning, I had breakfast with a group of people, including the documentary recording engineer, Ed Wolfrum, and Motown producer Clay McMurray. Johnny was supposed to have joined us. He never made it. As time marches on, it seems like I am losing more and more of my friends and contemporaries.

In early October of 2002, after my work with the Motown documentary was over, I received another exciting telephone call, this time from T. J. Lubinsky, the producer of the doo-wop specials on public television. It just so happens that I'd seen every one of them and really enjoyed his work.

T. J. was calling to invite me to play guitar with Pure Gold, the house band on the next special. It was to be called Love, Rhythm, and Soul, and would feature some of the biggest acts in R&B music history: Aretha Franklin, Lou Rawls, Dennis Edwards and the Temptations Review, the Spinners, Jerry Butler, Mary Wilson and the Supremes, Gloria Gaynor, Edwin Starr, the Originals, Barbara Mason, Peaches & Herb, Freda Payne, Carl Carlton, Blue Magic, the Three Degrees, Billy Paul, the Hues Corporation, Thelma Houston, and the Manhattans.

I arrived in Pittsburgh a day before rehearsal, and the bass player from the house band was there to pick me up at the airport.

Don, the guitar player with Pure Gold, had a professional recording studio, and we arrived there to rehearse. Don introduced me to the other guys in the band and gave me a tour of his studio. I got my guitar out, and we started to run over the songs. After playing awhile, I noticed something strange: everyone had a music chart in front of him except me. I asked Don where my charts were. He told me there weren't any rhythm charts. The members of the band learned the records by ear and created their own. He then offered to let me read from his charts, which were covered with numbers, like in the Nashville Numbering System. I had seen this kind of chart only once before, years ago when I'd recorded in Muscle Shoals with Wilson Pickett. I told Don that I'd keep playing by ear. I felt like the only man in a hatchet fight who hadn't been given a hatchet.

I got through most of the songs that day. Some of them I'd recorded to begin with, so it was just like old times. At the end of the rehearsal I asked Don to stay over and help me write some quick arrangements for myself. When we were done, the limo arrived and drove me back to the hotel. It felt just like being a star again.

The next day I got up early, practiced my guitar parts, and then went down to the hotel lobby to get a limo to take me to the rehearsal. But there was a mixup, and when I finally arrived at the theater and went up to the rehearsal area I was late and they had started without me. The bass player joked and said they thought I was so mad about not having any charts that I'd gone back to Detroit.

There was a complete string section sitting behind me with violins, violas, and cellos. On the other side of the stage, there was a complete horn section with trumpets, trombones, and saxophones.

That night the Benedum Theater was absolutely magnificent! They had three digital recording consoles linked together in the basement and a complete digital video system upstairs with camera booms attached to the walls of the theater. I could see people in rows all the way up to the ceiling.

Halfway through the show, T.J. introduced me to the audience.

"Now I would like to give credit where credit is due," he began, as he turned and pointed at me. "I would like to introduce you to guitarist Dennis Coffey. Dennis has played on many records at Motown. He has also played with Freda Payne and also had a hit record called 'Scorpio'," he continued. "Stand up, Dennis, and play us a few of those hot licks."

I stood up and played a few guitar licks for the crowd using my wah-wah pedal. The huge crowd erupted into applause. Man, it just doesn't get any better than this, I thought. Here I was again, hitting a few notes and having a wonderful time on a show with some of the greatest recording artists of the sixties and seventies.

The show was fantastic that night, and the crowd was dancing in the aisles in front of the stage. For the finale, Mary Wilson and Johnny Bristol sang the Supremes' hit "Some Day We'll Be Together." I had played on the original record, so to me it seemed like a great way to wrap up the show. I played my guitar part with the orchestra, and Mary and Johnny sang. Then everyone came onstage and joined in. It was a touching moment, and I was really glad to be there.

FARMINGTON, 2003

In March 2003, I visited Motown Studio A again, this time with my London publishers, Mike Ritson and Stuart Russell from BeeCool Publishing. We separated ourselves from the guides, and I gave them my own tour.

A short while later the rest of the group caught up with us, and the tour guides directed us in singing "My Girl" and doing hand claps and dance steps in the studio. They told us we could tell our friends we'd sung in the same Motown Studio as the Temptations. As we left the studio, I noticed that those vibes I had felt when I came into the studio a few years ago were no longer there.

I am currently shopping my new CD, *Flight of the Phoenix.* I now have a digital twenty-four-track recording studio in a room at my house, which I use for recording my new songs. I am also currently working on new projects and still doing what I love.

In addition to the equipment I donated to the Motown Museum, I've lent my Gibson Firebird guitar to the Henry Ford Museum. It was displayed in their new Motown exhibit for three years. I also have a copy of the "Scorpio" sheet music, a wah-wah pedal, and a fuzz tone on display at the Rock & Roll Hall of Fame and Museum in Cleveland, Ohio. "The Rock & Roll Kid" now has an official place in music history.

Selected Discography

DENNIS COFFEY—GUITAR AND/OR
PRODUCER/ARRANGER/WRITER—SONGS

Eighth Day	She's Not Just Another Woman	Invictus
	You've Got to Crawl (Before You Walk)	Invictus
100 Proof (Aged in Soul)	Somebody's Been Sleeping in My Bed	Hot Wax
	Too Many Cooks Spoil the Soup	Hot Wax
Paul Anka	Goodnight My Love	RCA
Darrel Banks	Open the Door to Your Heart	Revilot
J. J. Barnes	Day Tripper	Ric-Tic
	Real Humdinger	Ric-Tic
	Say It	Ric-Tic
Johnny Bristol	Hang On In There Baby	MGM
C. J. and Company	Devil's Gun	Westbound
	Big City Sidewalk	Westbound
	Free to Be Me	Westbound
	Deadeye Dick	Westbound
	We Got Our Own Thing Parts 1&2	Westbound
Little Carl Carlton	Competition Ain't Nothing	Back Beat
Jerry Carr	I'll Be Your Piece of the Rock	Cherie
Chairmen of the Board	Everything's Tuesday	Invictus
	Give Me Just a Little More Time	Invictus
	Pay the Piper	Invictus
	Finders Keepers	Invictus
	You've Got Me Dangling on a String	Invictus
	Patches	Invictus
Jamie Coe	The Fool	Enterprise
Dramatics	In the Rain	Volt
	What You See Is What You Get	Volt

Fantastic Four	The Whole World Is a Stage	Ric-Tic
	Bring Your Own Funk	Westbound
	I Got to Have Your Love	Westbound
	Disco Pool Blues	Westbound
	If This Is Love	Westbound
Laura Lee	Woman's Love Rights	Hot Wax
Glass House	Crumbs Off the Table	Invictus
Flaming Embers	I'm Not My Brother's Keeper	Hot Wax
	Mind, Body and Soul	Hot Wax
	Westbound Number Nine	Hot Wax
	Stop the World and Let Me Off	Hot Wax
King Errisson	Manhattan Love Song	Westbound
	LA Bound	Westbound
Floaters	Float On	ABC
Four Tops	Still Waters Run Deep	Motown
	If I Were a Carpenter	Motown
Gallery	Big City Miss Ruth Ann	Sussex
	I Believe in Music	Sussex
	Nice to Be With You	Sussex
Marvin Gaye	That's the Way Love Is	Tamla
	I Want You	Tamla
Grandmaster Flash	The Official Adventures of Grandmaster Flash	Strut (Studio K7)
Holidays	I'll Love You Forever	Golden World
Honey Cone	One Monkey Don't Stop No Show	Hot Wax
	Stick Up	Hot Wax
	Want Ads	Hot Wax
Al Kent	You've Got to Pay the Price	Ric-Tic
Gladys Knight	Friendship Train	Soul
	If I Was Your Woman	Soul
	Nitty Gritty	Soul
Johnny Mathis	The Heart of a Woman	Columbia
Miracles	Do It Baby	Do It Baby

Jackie Moore	Time	Atlantic
	Something in a Look	Atlantic
Carlos Munro	Boogie up, Rock Down	Westbound
Harry Nilsson	At My Front Door	Rapple
Originals	Baby, I'm for Real	Soul
George Clinton and the Parliaments	(I Wanna) Testify	Revilot
Freda Payne	Band of Gold	Invictus
	Bring the Boys Home	Invictus
Wilson Pickett	Don't Knock My Love	Atlantic
	Fire and Water	Atlantic
Diana Ross and the Supremes	Someday We'll Be Together	Motown
Royaltones	Our Faded Love	Mala
	Mairzy Doats	Twirl
	Misty Sea	Mala
Del Shannon	Handy Man	Amy
	Do You Want to Dance	Amy
	Keep Searching	Amy
	Little Town Flirt	Big Top
	Move It on Over	Amy
Spinners	It's a Shame	Motown
Edwin Starr	S.O.S. (Stop Her on Sight)	Ric-Tic
	War	Gordy
Supremes	I'm Livin' in Shame	Motown
	Nathan Jones	Motown
Sylvers	Boogie Fever	Capitol
Johnny Taylor	Who's Making Love	Stax
Temptations	Ball of Confusion	Gordy
	Cloud Nine	Gordy
	Don't Let the Jones Get You Down	Gordy
	I Can't Get Next to You	Gordy
	I Wish It Would Rain	Gordy
	Just My Imagination	Gordy
	Psychedelic Shack	Gordy
	Runaway Child	Gordy

	Super Star	Gordy
Mike Theodore Orchestra	I Love the Way You Move	Westbound
Fonzie Thorton	Perfect Lover	RCA
Undisputed Truth	Smiling Faces	Gordy
Junior Walker & the All-Stars	These Eyes	Soul
	What Does It Take to Win Your Love	Soul
Stevie Wonder	We Can Work It Out	Talma
Shorty Long	Here Comes the Judge	Soul
Various Artists	70's Smash Hits—Volume 5	Rhino
Various Artists	The Best of Impact Records	Collectables
Various Artists	Funk Hits	Double Play
Various Artists	Rock & Roll Reunion: Class of 71	Madacy Records
Various Artists	Sweet Taste of Sin: Sensual Break Beat Soul	BGP
Young Sisters	Playgirl	Twirl
	She Took His Love Away	Mala

DENNIS COFFEY—SESSION GUITAR—ALBUMS

Date	Artist	Title	Label
1963	Del Shannon	Del Shannon Sings Hank Williams	Big Top
1964	Shades of Blue	Happiness Is the Shades of Blue	Impact
1968	Mutzie	Light of Your Shadow	Sussex
1968	Amish	Amish	Sussex
1968	Rodriguez	Cold Fact	Sussex
1968	Jerry Butler	Soul Goes on	Mercury
1970	Edwin Starr	Hell up in Harlem	Motown
1971	Valerie Simpson	Valerie Simpson Exposed	Motown
1972	Gallery	Nice to Be With You	Sussex
1972	Four Tops	Nature Planned It	Motown

1973	Jimmy Ruffin	Jimmy Ruffin	Polydor
1974	Quincy Jones	Body Heat	A&M
1974	Lonnett Mckee	Lonnett	Motown
1974	Martha Reeves	Martha Reeves	MCA
1974	Ringo Starr	Goodnight Vienna	Apple
1975	Arthur Adams	Home Brew	Fantasy
1975	Eric Mercury	Eric Mercury	Mercury
1975	Yvonne Fair	Bitch Is Black	Motown
1976	Geoff Muldaur	Motion	Reprise
1976	Dramatics	Joy Ride	ABC
1976	Marvin Gaye	I Want You	Motown
1976	King Errisson	The Magic Man	Westbound
1976	Wilson Pickett	Greatest Hits	Atlantic
1977	Dramatics	Shake It Well	ABC
1977	King Errisson	LA Bound	Westbound
1977	Fantastic Four	I Got to Have Your Love	Westbound
1977	Jim Gold	I Can't Face Another Day	Sussex
1977	Larry Santos	Don't Let the Music Stop	Evolution
1978	Jim Gold	Home Town Hero	Sussex
1978	Fantastic Four	Bring Your Own Funk	Westbound
1979	Tempest Trio	Tempest Trio	Columbia
1980	Boz Scaggs	Hits	Columbia
1981	High Fashion	High Fashion	Capitol
1984	Rare Earth	Dreams/Answers	Motown
1992	Wilson Pickett	Man and a Half	Atlantic
1992	Hitsville	Hitsville USA	Motown
1994	Temptations	Emperors of Soul	Motown
1995	Marvin Gaye	Master 1961–1984	Motown
1995	Marvin Gaye	Classics Collection	Motown
1995	Best of TK Disco	Best of TK Disco	TK
1997	Shades of Blue	Golden Classics	Collectibles
1997	Gladys Knight	Ultimate Collection	Motown
1997	Junior Walker	Ultimate Collection	Motown
1998	Ultimate Motown	Rarities Collection	Motown
1998	Ultimate Motown	Rarities Volume	Motown
1998	Martha and the Vandellas	Ultimate Collection	Motown

1998	Marvelettes	Ultimate Collection	Motown
1998	Smokey Robinson	Ultimate Collection	Motown
1999	Pulp Fusion	Revenge of the Ghetto Grooves	MCA
2000	Ghostface Killah	Supreme Clientele	Sony
2001	Rage Against the Machine	Renegades	Epic
2003	Marvin Gayle	I Want You	Motown

Early Years and Northern Soul

Artist	Title	Label
Johnny Allen	EveryBody's Got a Girl but Me	Amy
Darrell Banks	Open the Door to Your Heart	Revilot
Duke Browner	Crying Over You	Impact
	Nothing But Love	Impact
Casual-Aires	You Know You Didn't Mean It	Enterprise
	The Millionaire	Enterprise
Mickey Denton	Now I'm Mister Blue	Amy
Mickey Denton	Mi Amore	Impact
	Don't Throw My Toys Away	World Artists
Don and Juan	I Can't Help Myself	Mala
Doomsday Machine	Where Sally Waits	Dot
Ricky Drapkin	Hey Come On And Dance	Patlow
King Errisson	LA Bound (album)	Sussex
	The Magic Man (album)	Sussex
Fantastic Four	Girl Have Pity	Ric-Tic
	To Share Your Love	Ric-Tic
	As Long As I Live	Ric-Tic
Tommy Frontera	Street of Shame	Palmer
Vic Gallon	I'm Gone	Gondola
Johnny Gibson Trio	Swanky	Twirl
Gunyun	Salvation Part 1	Dearborn
	Salvation Part 2	Dearborn
Holidays	No Greater Love	Golden World
Inner Circle	Sally Go Round the Roses	Impact
Irene and the Scotts	Why do You Treat Me Like You Do	Smash

	I'm Stuck on My Baby	Smash
Johnny and the Hurricanes	It's a Mad Mad World	Mala
	Money Honey	Mala
Al Kent	Finders Keepers	Ric-Tic
Theresa Lindsey	I'll Bet You	Golden World
	Daddy-O	Golden World
Lonette	Mind Intruder	Dearborn
	DNIM REDURTNI	Dearborn
	Stop, Don't Worry About it	Dearborn
Magnetics	Lady in Green	Bonnie
George McCannon III	Love, Love, My Friend	DynoVoice
Tony Michaels	Picture Me and You	Golden World
	I Love the Life I Live	Golden World
Jock Mitchell	You May Lose the One You Love	Impact
Jack Montgomery	Dearly Beloved	Scepter
	Don't Turn Your Back on Me	Barracuda
Monticellos	Don't Hold Back	Red Cap
	I Can't Wait to See My Baby's Face	Red Cap
Nabay	Believe It or Not	Impact
Nick & Dino	Boy	Impact
Kris Peterson	Me Without You	Pelikin
	I Believe in You	Pelikin
Jimmy Rand	Peggy Peggy	Madison
Johnny Rand	Still in my Heart	Herald
Anthony Raye	Give Me One More Chance	Impact
Michael and Raymond	Man without a Woman	RCA
San Remo Strings	Festival Time	Ric-Tic
	International Love Theme	Ric-Tic
John Rhys and the Lively Set	Nothing But Love	Impact
Rodriguez	Cold Fact	Sussex

Royaltones	Misty Sea	Mala
	Lonely World	Mala
Bobby Rydell	Our Faded Love	Cameo
Dave Sandy	Going Swimmin'	Twirl
Bob Santa Maria	I've Cried My Last Tear	Volkano
Scott Brothers	Got to Get a Groove	Smash
	My Day Has Come	Smash
Shades of Blue	How Do You Save a Dying Love?	Impact
	Lonely Summer	Impact
Shirley and the Sweethearts	Tony	Twirl
	Until You Tried Love	Twirl
Shondells	Everybody's Talkin'	Challenge
Bobbie Smith	Miss Strong Hearted	American Arts
	Walk on into My Heart	American Arts
Bobby Smith and the Creations	This Is Love	Ember
Strides	I Can Get Along	The Strides
	The Stride	The Strides
	Make Your Move	Dearborn
	I'm So Glad We're Together	Dearborn
Sunliners	Land of Nod	MGM
Terry and the Topics	Just a Gigolo	Coral
Theo-Coff Invasion	Lucky Day	Dearborn
Volcanos	A Lady's Man	Arctic
Volumes	I Got Love	Twirl
Monkey Hop	Old Town	
	My Road Is the Right Road	Inferno
	My Kind of Girl	Inferno
	Gotta Give Her Love	American Arts
	I Can't Live Without You	American Arts
	I Just Can't Help Myself	American Arts
	One Way Lover	American Arts
	Oh My Mother-in-law and Our Song	Jubilee

	That Same Old Feeling	Impact
	The Trouble I've Seen	Impact
Maurice Williams	Come and Get It	Herald
Danny Woods	To Be Loved	Smash
	Come On and Dance Part 2	Smash
Patti Young	Head and Shoulders	Ernstrat

Music Gear

The equipment I used early in my musical journey was as follows.

First guitar	Old Hawaiian slide guitar, which I spray painted myself and had converted to a regular Spanish guitar. Cost—free; it was given to me.
Second guitar	Harmony acoustic purchased for me by my dad from a pawnshop in downtown Detroit—cost $15.
First electric guitar	Harmony Electric—an acoustic with a small pickup and two control knobs for volume and tone—cost $35.
Small amp	Name unknown.
First large amp	Magnatone Tremelo.
Second electric guitar	Premier cutaway—two pickups, four controls for volume and tone, and pickup selector toggle switch. Color—all black with sparkles. I used this on my first record date at the age of fifteen—"I'm Gone" by Vic Gallon on Gondola Records.

LATER YEARS

Third electric guitar	Orange Chet Atkins model, Gretsch.
Second amp	Fender Bassman with four ten-inch speakers.
First distortion device	Loosened tube in an amp at Bell Sound in New York while recording with the

	Royaltones for Harry Balk (the recording engineer filtered out all of the distortion because he thought it was a technical problem).
Fourth electric guitar	Guild—also used when working with the Royaltones.
Next amp for gigs	Fender Super Reverb (also used with Fender Power Speaker cabinet with ten-inch speakers for concerts).
Additional amps	Marshall head and Sunn bottom used in concerts, Fender 75 and Music Man 112 RD used for club gigs, Fender Princeton Reverb used for sessions in Detroit and L.A.
Fifth electric guitar	Gibson Byrdland—new, 1963—used on live jazz/funk gigs and first album *Hair And Thangs* on Sussex Records.
Sixth electric guitar	Gibson Firebird—used, 1964—used on the album *Evolution* on Sussex Records and on all Motown and Northern Soul records. Used on my last CD, *Under The Moonlight,* on Orpheus Records.
Seventh electric guitar	Fender Stratocaster—used on *Going For Myself* album on Sussex.
Eighth electric guitar	Gibson Les Paul—used at concerts.
Ninth electric guitar	Used, 1973—Gibson red 345 stereo converted to mono with added pickup out of phase switch—used on L.A. sessions and *Instant Coffey* album.
Additional guitar	Gibson acoustic—also used on *Evolution* album.
Additional guitar	Guild 12 acoustic twelve string—used on L.A. sessions.
Additional guitar	Coral electric sitar—used on Freda Payne's "Band Of Gold."

ACCESSORIES

Cry Baby wah-wah pedal	First used on "Cloud Nine" by the Temptations
Echoplex	First used on intro to "In The Rain" by the Dramatics
Vox tone bender	Used on many records for distortion
Assorted MXR, Electro Harmonic, and Peavey pedals Hammond Condor unit	Used on solo for "Smiling Faces Sometimes" by the Undisputed Truth, Wilson Pickett's "Don't Knock My Love," and other records
Echoplex, wah-wah, and tone bender	Used on "Ball Of Confusion," "Psychedelic Shack," and "Runaway Child" by the Temptations
Sho Bud volume pedal	Used on sessions in L.A.
Line 6 pod effects	Used now for sessions
Boss pedals: distortion, digital delay, chorus, and blues distortion pedal	Use now

Strings: Ernie Ball 10 Regular Slinky for electric guitar, Martin Marquis Light for acoustic guitar, GHS La Classique or Albert Augustine LTD for classical guitar

CURRENT EQUIPMENT

Guitars, old favorites	Gibson 335, Gibson 345, Gibson Firebird, and Gibson Byrdland
Guitars, new	Hondo acoustic guitar and Washburn classical electric guitar
Amplifiers	Music Man 112 RD, Polytone Mini Brute IV, and Peavey Bandit 65

MAGAZINE ARTICLES AND BOOKS

Dennis Coffey Guitar Warner Brothers Publications, 1972
Guitar Player Magazine December 1973, December 1988
Standing in the Shadows of Motown: The Life and Music of Legendary Bassist James Jamerson, by Allan Slutsky Dr. Licks Publishing, 1989
DISCoveries Issue 74, July 1994
Big Daddy Quarterly Issue 8, October 2001
Manifesto June 2002
Mojo Magazine January 2003

LIVE TV SHOWS

American Bandstand
In-Concert with the Temptations
Mike Douglas
Soul Train
The Real Don Steele
Midnight Special
Rhythm, Love, and Soul, Public Broadcasting (PBS), 2002

MOVIES

Standing in the Shadows of Motown
Radio Revolution: The Rise and Fall of the Big 8